BUFFALO
Music Learning Theory
Resolutions and Beyond

Also by Edwin E. Gordon, available from GIA Publications, Inc.

A Music Learning Theory for Newborn and Young Children
Learning Sequences in Music
The Psychology of Music Teaching
Study Guide for Learning Sequences in Music
The Nature, Description, Measurement, and Evaluation of Music Aptitudes
Designing Objective Research in Music Education
The Musical Aptitude Profile
The Iowa Tests of Music Literacy
Primary Measures of Music Audiation
Intermediate Measures of Music Audiation
Advanced Measures of Music Audiation
Guiding Your Child's Music Development
Audie
Am I Musical: Discover Your Music Potential
Rhythm: Contrasting the Implications of Audiation and Notation
Introduction to Research and the Psychology of Music
Preparatory Audiation, Audiation, and Music Learning Theory
Rating Scales and Their Uses for Measuring and Evaluating Achievement in Music Performance
Harmonic Improvisation for Adult Musicians
Music Education Research: Taking a Panoptic Measure of Reality
Discovering Music from the Inside Out: An Autobiography
Improvisation in the Music Classroom
The Aural/Visual Experience of Music Literacy

BUFFALO

Music Learning Theory

Resolutions and Beyond

Edwin E. Gordon
Research Professor
University of South Carolina

GIA Publications, Inc.
Chicago

G-6866

7404 S. Mason Ave., Chicago, IL 60638
www.giamusic.com

Layout: Robert M. Sacha

ISBN-10: 1-57999-594-2
ISBN-13: 978-1-5799-9594-2

Printed in the U.S.A.

Table of Contents

Introduction

Widespread use of the word curriculum in education is well understood. It derives from the Latin *currere*, which means to establish a course, to run. Historically, curriculum was closely related to *current*, suggesting steady, smooth onward movement, as in flowing from one to another. What is intended to progress steadily within an educational curriculum is sequential presentation of subject matter, each component serving as readiness for flowing into higher ones.

In reading and arithmetic curriculums, for example, sequential presentation of progressively complex skills and knowledge is delineated for students who are expected to advance successfully in those subjects. Unfortunately, that is rarely the case with music curriculums. With regard to students who are receiving classroom instruction in music, philosophers argue about whether listening or performance should be paramount. Attention to developing audiation, which is fundamental to musical listening and performance, is summarily dismissed. Thus, institutionalized curriculums are usually based on extra-musical considerations, which in themselves encompass no sequential imperatives and thus rarely are presented in an orderly and serious manner. Entertainment rather than education takes center stage, with leadership in music education focused timidly on demands of the public. This may be validated by lending an ear to the so much loud unenlightened repetitious and endlessly boring sounds in the environment referred to by those with unrefined ears as music discharged by musicians. Whatever trivial music might emanate is subordinate to the social commentary of the words, suggesting a contemporary type of soap opera characterized by extraneous reverberations surrounding the lyric. In a passion for vulgarity, listeners mouth empty words with exaggerated movement, and any attempt to render a melodic line is woefully insufficient and subdued by trendy electronics and visual images. Certainly more should be possible given systematic music instruction in the schools, and those with extraordinary music potential who find it necessary to struggle to release their capabilities would with ease necessarily contribute considerably more to culture.

Music learning theory was conceived to diminish this described plight. Based on years of empirical, observational, and experimental research, music learning theory is designed to provide explanations of how we learn music. Emphasis is on what is taught, why it is taught, and when it is taught. Most important, however, is *when* something is taught so it may appropriately serve as sequential readiness for learning more complex knowledge and skills. How to teach rightfully belongs in the domain of teaching. Whereas learning is from the inside out and teaching is from the outside in, a music learning theory curriculum takes direction from understanding the sequential nature of how students learn, not from how teachers themselves were taught or how teachers were taught to teach. Tending to students' individual musical needs by adapting instruction to their normative and idiographic music aptitude differences, as determined by objective results derived from valid developmental and stabilized music aptitude tests along with tenets of sequential learning and audiation, is integral to music learning theory.

Music Learning Theory

We learn in two generic ways: discrimination and inference. Discrimination learning is fundamental because it provides necessary readiness for inference learning, which is the more conceptual of the two. However, discrimination and inference learning are not mutually exclusive. They occur together as one or the other receives greater emphasis. As with learning a language, imitation is crucial readiness for discrimination learning. It provides bases for generalization and abstraction that occur later in audiation, during inference learning. We make only simple inferences as we engage in discrimination learning, but we use much, if not all, we have discriminated as we engage in inference learning. Students engage in discrimination learning when they are conscious of being taught, but do not fully understand what they are being taught or why they are being taught it. For example, when students learn to sing through imitation, or when they perform music after memorizing it from a score, they engage in discrimination learning, because, in addition to other proficiencies, they learned to discriminate among pitches and durations. On the other hand, inference learning occurs when students are unconscious of what they are learning or that they are learning, because they are teaching themselves to learn what is unfamiliar by inferring from what is familiar. The more facts and ideas students discriminate among, the more inferences they are able to make. Though a teacher cannot teach students what to infer, a teacher can teach students not only how best to discriminate, but how to teach themselves to make inferences. In other words, although a teacher can teach students both how and what to discriminate, a teacher can only guide students in how to make inferences.

Audiation

Sound itself is not music. Sound becomes music through audiation, when as listening in language you translate sounds in your mind and give them meaning. The meaning you give to these sounds will be different depending on the occasion, as well as different from meanings given them by other persons. Audiation is the process of assimilating and comprehending (not simply rehearing) music we have just heard performed or have heard performed sometime in the past. We also audiate when we assimilate and comprehend music we may or may not have heard, but are reading in notation or composing or improvising. In contrast, aural perception takes place when we are actually hearing sound the moment it is being produced. We audiate actual sound only after we have aurally perceived it. In aural perception we are dealing with immediate sound events, whereas in audiation, we are dealing with delayed music events. Moreover, compared to what is often called music imagery, audiation is a more profound process. Music imagery casually suggests a vivid or figurative picture of what music might represent. It does not require assimilation and comprehension of music as does audiation.

Learning Sequence Activities

Music learning theory provides the conceptual basis for practical applications of learning sequence activities. Learning sequence activities take place during the first few minutes of a class period or rehearsal, and customary classroom or performance activities account for the remainder of class time. When *Jump Right In: The Music Curriculum* and *Jump Right In: The Instrumental Series* were written, primary concern was with young students who were in beginning or initial stages of music instruction. Thus, how a teacher might begin to use learning sequence activities with older students, those in middle and senior high school who had received traditional music instruction in elementary school, was slighted. That issue has intermittently come to my attention, but it became patently obvious while I was conducting a two-week summer seminar at the State University of New York-Buffalo in 2005. Teachers required special assistance in understanding how to use learning sequence activities with students who, for example, were taught to name individual pitches and durations but were not guided in contextually audiating tonal, rhythm, and harmonic patterns. That situation is analogous to reciting letters of the alphabet but not having familiarity with words. Further, students taught traditionally typically have no idea of what unfamiliar and perhaps familiar notation sounds like until they hear its physical sound. And although most music students are able to decode music notation and render it on a music instrument, they lack readiness to engage in music improvisation, the mainstay of audiation. Teachers who acknowledge compelling benefits of learning sequence activities have specifically requested curricular guidance in shepherding students through transitional processes to and from traditional instruction to and from instruction based on music learning theory. That is the primary purpose of the book.

Organization of the Content

There are six parts to the book. Part 1 is a discussion of the interaction of movement and breathing as readiness for students to learn rhythm regardless of the nature of their past music achievement. The distinction between musical time and space is explained. Experiencing space, which both younger and older students are routinely denied, serves as foundation for comprehending musical time in learning sequence activities. Part 2 is a practical explanation of how elementary school instrumental students who have been taught in terms of learning sequence activities may transitionally relate their skills and knowledge to traditional music terminology later in common-practice instruction. Part 3 deals with adapting learning sequence activities to middle and senior high school instrumental students who have had only routine music instruction. Part 4 is similar to Part 3 but it is directed toward choral students. Part 5 details how new students in a class may be integrated with ease into learning sequence activities, how learning sequence activities may be used successfully in combined-grades classroom music in which some students have achieved advanced units while others students have had exposure to only introductory units, and proposes suggestions for record keeping. Part 6 explains how learning sequence activities may enhance audiation of adult musicians in colleges and universities.

Information about music learning theory, audiation, and learning sequence activities not addressed herein may be found in *Learning Sequences in Music: A Contemporary Music Learning Theory*. With regard to music aptitude, music aptitude testing, and improvisation, read *Introduction to Research and the Psychology of Music*, *Improvisation in the Music Classroom*, and *Harmonic Improvisation for Adult Musicians*. These books, among others of mine, are listed in the Bibliography.

Part I

Movement and Interactive Breathing as Readiness for Learning Rhythm

It seems students have been taught forever to count numbers as a means of learning rhythm. Whomever the persons who initiated and sustained the idea, they have unintentionally impaired music education at all levels of instruction. The primary problem is students may correctly name numbers but they do not always recite them at appropriate times. Although music theory is explained to them, parallel rhythmic feeling is lacking. Teachers often suggest foot tapping, but that exacerbates the problem. Foot muscles become tense and tempos unsteady. The undesirable situation grows obvious as tempos rush and slow and individual notes are given improper duration. Thus, rhythm is distorted. Perhaps most egregious is when rests are counted. As a rule, performance after a rest is begun too late or too early. Moreover, students are often stopped and corrected if an incorrect pitch is performed, even when it is performed with correct rhythm, but teachers rarely are concerned when students' rhythm is incorrect if it is performed with correct pitches.

The impediment to counting might be more thoroughly explained this way. Students are taught time before they are guided in experiencing space. It is the feeling of space through body movement that indicates to students when consecutive beats are to occur. Counting is unnecessary, if not counterproductive. Once students are comfortable moving in space with supportive breath, either by standing in place or moving around the room and activating upper and/or lower parts of their body, they begin to impose musical time on space. That is accomplished by internalizing the feeling of space as beats are properly placed in the flow of musical time. In a word, no longer moving in a organized manner, students "audiate" space as they perform rhythm in accordance with placement of beats. Soon energy is added to students' unique movement in terms of artistic verve, and that contributes to a comprehensive understanding of rhythm and musicianship. Although it is said there are five senses — seeing, smelling, tasting, touching, and feeling — there is at least one more sense: moving. Kinesthesia detects body movement and position in terms of muscles, tendons, and joints. The four subparts of kinesthesia, using Rudolf Laban's translated German words, are time, space, weight, and flow.

Regardless of whether students are familiar with or new to music learning theory and learning sequence activities, for maximum achievement it is recommended they be introduced in sequential order, from first to last, to the twenty-four melodies and accompanying suggestions for guiding students' movement. However, a time schedule for introducing each melody is arbitrary. Depending upon age of students, number of classes in the semester or year, length of class periods and time devoted to movement activities in each period, and to what extent movement instruction is combined with traditional instruction during a given period, only some rather than all melodies may be given attention. If only a few melodies can be performed due to workaday restraints, even the first four, in which only upper parts of the body are used to explore space, should prove beneficial in providing at least a firm foundation for learning rhythm. In a class designed for adult musicians as well as amateurs in which movement is the sole concern, perhaps instruction using all twenty-four melodies may cover more than one year. Whatever the circumstances, you will find it advantageous to scan the entire set of melodies and pedagogical suggestions before any instruction is initiated. The synopsis should be not only informative, it also will assist you in preparing students in making smooth and comfortable transitions from melody to melody.

Elongations, ties, rests, and upbeats in music are best suited for guiding students in moving their body in space before they are expected to demonstrate skill in accordance with flow, weight, and time. Rather than explaining how that is accomplished in ongoing text, I have determined it would be more productive to present twenty-four specially composed short, simple melodies incorporating elongations, ties, rests, and upbeats with specific suggestions for spatial movement. Twenty melodies are in major and harmonic minor tonalities and either usual duple, triple or combined meters; two are in Dorian and Mixolydian tonalities; and two are in unusual paired and unpaired meters. Although suggestions are designed specifically for individual melodies, many of the same ideas, because of their fundamental importance, are found in several melodies. Also, inclusive discussions about rhythm are offered in addition to suggestions for guiding students' movement. Of course, it is anticipated the melodies presented will be supplemented with extant melodies or others you might compose.

It will be discovered a tie is a distinct type of elongation. Whereas an elongation connects macrobeats, microbeats, or divisions of microbeats within a single rhythm pattern, a tie connects macrobeats, microbeats, or divisions of microbeats between rhythm patterns. A rhythm pattern in usual meter and unusual paired meter embodies two contiguous macrobeats within a rhythm pattern. Three contiguous macrobeats constitute a rhythm pattern in unusual unpaired meter. Rests and upbeats require no special explanation. However, to assist students in developing free-flowing continuous movement in space, it will prove helpful to remember a rest is not silent, it is attached in audiation to the melodic pattern it precedes or follows. Further, upbeats are not found only at the beginning of a melody. They may occur anywhere throughout a melody.

Overview of the Melodies

The concepts presented in this overview are general. Not all are expected to apply to every melody. Judiciousness in their appropriate and timely application is left to your sensitive and thoughtful discretion. Some concepts are selectively reinforced and others are introduced to complement relevant and more specific pedagogical procedures outlined in association with each melody. Whatever the case, students need ample physical space to appropriately participate in movement activities. They should be able to stretch both arms in all directions without touching anything or anyone else. Thus, if instruction takes place in a room with unmovable desks, a gymnasium or auditorium stage might better be used. Weather permitting, moving outdoors may be a promising alternative. Any ample location is acceptable because equipment to play cassettes or CDs is not necessary. If a physical education or other teacher has background in Laban or Dalcroze methodologies, and thus an interest in movement, especially modern dance, she or he may be invited to join, if not assist in teaching, the class.

None of the melodies are intended to be performed with words. When words are used, students normally focus on the text, and as a result music itself becomes of secondary importance. Moreover, words tend to permissively encourage uncertain singers to use a speaking voice quality rather than a singing voice quality. Neutral syllables, such as *bah*, *lah*, *mah*, *dah*, serve well. These syllables are positioned in front of the mouth, not in the throat, and are comfortably and easily expressed with minimal movement of lips and tongue.

It will be noticed Roman-numeral chord-symbols are indicated above all melodies. They are for accompaniment and improvisatory purposes. When used to assist students in learning a melody, chords without melody are played on a guitar, baritone ukulele, or piano. If the melody is played, students will tend to memorize rather than audiate the melody. Instrumental chordal accompaniments may be used as a melody is being learned as well as after students have learned the melody and movement is begun. When students are inclined to engage in improvisation, it will be apparent harmonic improvisation offers direction to and enriches elegant and agile movement. Specific suggestions pertaining to inclusion of harmonic improvisation in movement activities are offered for several melodies. For example, one group of students may sing chords as another group is improvising a melody based on a chord progression while other are moving in a free-flowing continuous manner. The harmonic indications are arbitrary and, of course, may be supplemented or changed as you see fit.

Before guiding students in moving to a melody, I recommend you become familiar with the melody by singing it several times. So as not to need to make reference to notation as movement is undertaken, familiarity is important. Once a musical interpretation is decided upon with special attention given to phrasing and a satisfactory tempo, sing the melody and encourage students to move in accompaniment. Initially, students do not sing as they are moving. However, initially combining singing with movement may offer direction to mature students for acquiring more graceful movement, those who already move comfortably and effortlessly to melodies performed by others. Either way, all students might sing the melody in ensemble or solo before they begin moving to it. Moreover, it may be befitting for you and students together to chant the rhythm of the melody, using the same pitch throughout with inflection and dynamics so full mindfulness may be given to movement. After students are at ease with free-flowing continuous movement, they may sing the melody as accompaniment to their movement. Note: neither you nor students engage in dancing, conducting, or counting when moving in a free-flowing continuous manner. To do so countermands freedom of movement and unintentionally shifts emphasis from space to time.

As readiness for free-flowing continuous movement, you might placidly model gentle movement of the head, neck, and shoulders for students. Deep breaths are fundamental to all types of movement, and they are taken before and in conjunction with movement itself. Without ample inhalation and exhalation, movement will be stiff and lactic acid will not be emitted from muscles. Unless these three parts of the body, which are usually tense, are relaxed, appropriate movement with the remainder of the body will be restrained. Care and sufficient time is necessary to insure movement from shoulders up is not rigid. Slow and deliberate movement in this endeavor is most effective.

It has been my experience types of movement presented herein work well with young children, those in preschool through grade three. However, beginning sometime in grade four, students, boys in particular, tend to become embarrassed by spatial movement. Many associate femininity with the motions. Moreover, many older students, because of lack of coordination, are too self-conscious to participate in movement activities directed toward assisting them in maintaining musical time in their rhythmic development. Conflicting attitudes may be overcome when you are persistent and not demanding. Should you give the impression you are unsure or doubtful, that will encourage students to act likewise. That attitude can be averted by you confidently modeling movements to be undertaken by students without apology or justification.

Begin with modest movements, encouraging students who are self-assured and willing to partake without insisting lingerers participate. Particularly if one or more class leaders cooperate, in time others will follow. Perhaps best advice might be for you and/or the class to create games in which four or five students move together in separate groups. Students should not be led to believe the object of any game is to learn how to move. To the contrary, emphasis should be on rules of the game. For example, catching and throwing a ball or pretending an athletic game is being played, with the code being everyone at all times must be in continuous free-flowing movement. Whomever stops moving costs a team, preferably boys against girls, points. You or a student keeps score for all to see as the game proceeds. Patience on your part is a necessity. There will be some students whose coordination is so impoverished or rhythm aptitude so meek that imitating your model will be inordinately challenging. Nonetheless, all students who collaborate will be successful in terms of their own potential, and that is important. Regardless of chronological age and whether transitioning into or out of learning sequence activities, students continually experience movement in space to achieve and enjoy their foremost possibilities in musical time and rhythm.

A final few remarks may be in order. You, like many music educators, most likely received a traditional music education before, during, and after your college and university methods and music theory classes, student teaching experiences, and applied music lessons. Thus, knowledge and skills pertaining to audiation, tonal and rhythm solfege, and movement are probably not as ambiguous as note letter-names, note-value names, counting, and time and key signatures. Although you are assuredly adept at connecting instrumental fingerings with music notation, you must learn to be patient with yourself as you are exposed to concepts and skills associated with music learning theory and learning sequence activities. Have no doubt you will be learning along with your students. Expand your and their musicianship by embracing audiation, notational audiation, improvisation, and creativity.

Preparatory Relaxation Activities

1. Before students begin to move to a melody, it is advantageous for them to partake in preparatory relaxation activities. Music is not heard during these activities because if so, students will naturally tend to move in musical time. Students observe you model with comfort and ease movement of the head side to side, the return after a pause being made in a circular manner by shifting the head slightly up and down and down and up. In that way there will be continuous movement of the head. Only sympathetic, not purposeful, movement of the neck and shoulders takes place. After watching you, students imitate the movement. The activity is not rushed or labored. When you are convinced most if not all students are moving without tension, a segue to the next step is undertaken.
2. Appropriate movement and breathing are dependent on each other. Unless deep breaths are taken and air is released slowly without constraint in conjunction with movement, motion will not be relaxed and free-flowing. Strain in various parts of the body will result. When learning to breathe in this manner before movement to the melody is undertaken, students learn

to participate in proper movement with less modeling and instruction being necessary. Moreover, through this type of performance a byproduct of metabolism, lactic acid, is beneficially released from muscles.

3. As the head is in continuous rotation as before, it moves from side to side. Tension in the neck will be abated and head and neck movement will be balanced.
4. With head and neck still moving, shoulders alternating one at a time or together move in circular motion. Take care to be certain neither students' head, neck, nor shoulders are moving to beats in musical time, that is, with disconnected motion. Movement is always free-flowing and continuous. If physical tension seems to be occurring, the activity is stopped and students assume relaxed positions. Then, the activity, from head to shoulders, is begun once again. In all, only a few minutes is allocated to this action which is repeated the next time the class meets. Assuming physical tension is not present, reiteration cannot be overdone.

Melody 1

Melody 1 is in major tonality and usual triple meter. It is eight measures and includes tonic and dominant-seventh chords. Dotted-quarter notes = M.M. 60. Although the melody is in C keyality, it may be transposed as desired.

Pedagogy

1. Become familiar with Melody 1 and sing it to the group several times. Then the group sings along with you. Soon after the group is familiar with the melody, you no longer sing with them. Students sing the song, repeating it several times, as you move without singing in a free-flowing continuous manner but with deep breathing. That is, you model both appropriate movement and breathing students are to imitate.
2. The model students observe does not include or even suggest "keeping time" by pausing between macrobeats or accenting macrobeats. Meter is felt but not seen. Macrobeats and microbeats, of course, are audiated but not physically marked in performance. Musical expression occurs between macrobeats, not on them. Certainly movements do not include conducting, and in no way do movements indicate stylized or otherwise memorized dance steps for folk dancing. If anything, ballet motion is the rule, reference never being made to counting beats or musical time.
3. Most important is the way movement is fulfilled. For Melody 1, only upper parts of the body, from the waist up, are moved. That is, head, shoulders, neck, arms, hands, wrists, and chest move individually and/or in combination, with emphasis given to large muscle movement. It is with use of large muscles a necessary feeling of weight is acquired. Feet are firmly placed and legs are comfortably spread so the entire body ensures a center of weight and balance. Students do not move around the room. They maintain being anchored in their physical space.
4. As with the remaining melodies, Melody 1 is designed to liberate free-flowing continuous movement. Notice the ties attaching measures 1 and 2, 3 and 4, and 5 through 7. Continuous movement flows freely through each tie without any action to suggest placement of underlying macrobeats as several repetitions of the melody are performed.
5. Various types of expression and body dynamics (not sonic) may be visually apparent, particularly with regard to enunciating suitable but different arm and hand movements when an eighth note is tied to another eighth note as compared to when a

dotted-quarter note is tied to an eighth note. Also, differences between the two-measure phrases sharing the same rhythm (measures 1 to 2, 3 to 4, and 5 to 6) may be pronounced.

6. Advantage is taken of the opportunity to heighten a musical retardando as movement flows freely, continuously, and completely through a physical diminuendo to the dotted-half note in the final measure, affirming the beginning and ending of each rendition.
7. As you sing Melody 1 and move at the same time if desired, students move in accompaniment, emulating movement you have modeled or are modeling. All students may move together or alternate as one group sings and another moves. Finally, students may sing as they are moving.
8. Indicated tonic and dominant-seventh chord symbols, or alternate ones, may be followed as you or a student accompanies group singing using a chording instrument without marking macrobeats. Melody is always sung, not performed on an instrument. In the event an autoharp is used, special attention is given to accurate tuning.

Melody 2

Melody 2 is in harmonic minor tonality and usual duple meter. It is twelve measures and includes tonic, dominant-seventh, and subdominant chords. Quarter notes = M.M. 64. Although the melody is in C keyality, it may be transposed as desired.

Pedagogy

1. Review Preparatory Relaxation Activities.
2. Suggestions 1 through 3 for Melody 1 are also applicable to Melody 2. Only upper parts of the body are moved. Macrobeats and microbeats are not accented. Dancing, counting, and conducting jeopardize free-flowing continuous movement in initial stages of learning. With use of large muscles, a necessary feeling of weight is acquired. Feet are firmly placed and legs are comfortably spread so the entire body ensures a center of weight and balance. Deep breathing is continuous while moving.
3. As you model movement and breathing, students become aware tempo for usual duple meter may be somewhat faster than for usual triple meter. Also, although usual duple meter is more suggestive of musical time than space, marking macrobeats in musical time with any parts of the body is still avoided.
4. Contrasting movements are shaped in terms of using more and less space with various parts of the upper body to distinguish among longer and shorter durations. Different motion responses to groups of half, quarter, sixteenth, and thirty-second notes are pointed.
5. Movement takes place before singing during the sixteenth-notes rests at the beginning of measures 1 and 2. There might be a crescendo and retardando toward the sixteenth-notes after each rest.
6. Different physical dynamics distinguish between different structures of thirty-second notes in measures 4 and 8 and the same structure of thirty-second notes in measures 11 and 12.
7. Subdominant function in measure 9 may be considered by some to be associated with a dissonant melodic pitch while others might enjoy the sound as being richly consonant. Diverse movements may focus different interpretations.
8. The seeming coda might be expressively underscored with suggestive visual dynamics and various parts of the upper body

occupying different areas of space. Immediate repetition of measure 11 in measure 12 is made emphatic with firmness and restraint.

9. As you sing Melody 2 and move at the same time if desired, students move in accompaniment, emulating movement you modeled or are modeling. All students may move together or alternate as one group sings and another moves. Finally, all students may sing as they are moving.
10. Indicated tonic, dominant-seventh and subdominant chord symbols or alternate ones in harmonic minor tonality may be followed as you or a student accompany group singing using a chording instrument without marking macrobeats. Melody is always sung, not performed on an instrument. In the event an autoharp is used, give special attention to accurate tuning.

Melody 3

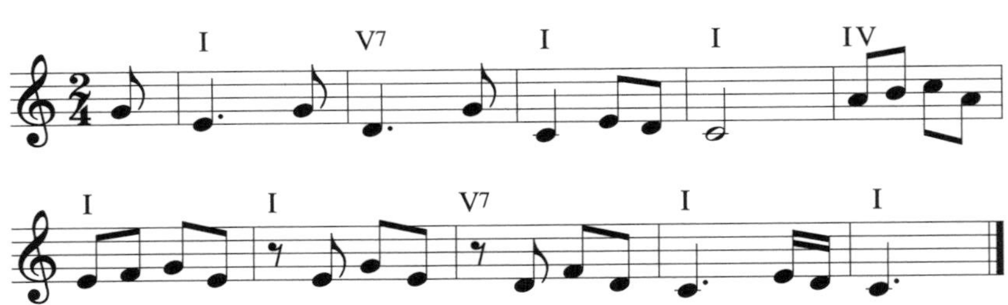

Melody 3 is in major tonality and usual duple meter. It is ten measures, incorporating upbeats and rests, and includes tonic, dominant-seventh, and subdominant chords. Quarter notes = M.M. 66. Although the melody is in C keyality, it may be transposed as desired.

Pedagogy

1. Review Preparatory Relaxation Activities.
2. Suggestions 1 through 3 for Melody 1 may be reviewed. Only upper parts of the body are put in motion.

3. Sing the melody a few times, pausing between repeats so placement of the initial upbeat is well understood by students.
4. Ask students to audiate the melody before they begin to move. Ample time is allotted so they may audiate the complete melody once as if it were actually being performed. Do not conduct or otherwise offer visible placement of beats. Students are encouraged to use their imagination as they are audiating and to think of creative movements to accompany the melody when they begin to move. When covert audiation flows smoothly into overt movement, students become less dependent on continually imitating your movements.
5. To create means to relate. With regard to movement, relationship is initiated inside the body (in the mind) and transferred to outside the body (to physical activity). The root meaning of *art* is to *fit together*. When we fit audiation to physical activity, we are creating.
6. Sing the melody twice without a pause. Students are instructed to begin moving in concert with the upbeat the second time the melody is begun. All students may move together or alternate as one group sings and another moves. Finally, all students sing as they are moving.
7. Especially when responding to the initial upbeat, a deep breath is taken as preparation. Artistry in expressive movement is dependent on quality of its preparation.
8. Upbeats are not confined to the beginning of a melody. In Melody 3, the eighth notes in measures 1 and 2 may be considered upbeats to patterns in following measures. Similarly, the two thirty-second notes may be audiated as an upbeat to the final dotted-quarter note. Upbeats become part of and stream into the melodic pattern they precede.
9. Students are guided in using varied motions to differentiate among upbeats as each is expressed with unique intentionality.
10. With regard to phrasing, only one deep breath is taken for the first four-measures, another for the next two measures, and another for the final four measures.

11. Rests are not actually rests, because energy in terms of weight and flow are evident in movement during musical silence. A rest becomes part of the melodic pattern it precedes or follows. A suitable type of movement underlying the two rests suggests agogic (not temporal) accents.
12. The thirty-second notes may be executed with staccato small muscle movements, perhaps using fingers, functioning as extensions of and in combination with legato free-flowing and continuous large muscle movement. To that extent, fingers might suggest musical time superimposed on spatial arm and hand movements.
13. The final dotted-quarter note is sustained with a crescendo as it flows naturally into the upbeat in repetitions of the melody.
14. Indicated tonic, dominant-seventh and subdominant chord symbols or alternate ones in major tonality may be followed as you or a student accompany group singing using a chording instrument without marking macrobeats. Melody is always sung, not performed on an instrument.

Melody 4

Melody 4 is in harmonic minor tonality and usual triple meter. It is eight measures and includes tonic, dominant-seventh, and subdominant chords. Dotted-quarter notes = M.M. 56. C keyality may be transposed.

Pedagogy

1. Review Preparatory Relaxation Activities.
2. Review suggestions 1 through 3 for Melody 1. Only upper parts of the body are moved.
3. As with Melody 3, ask students to audiate the melody before they begin to move. Ample time is allotted so students may audiate the complete melody once as if it were actually being performed. Do not conduct or otherwise offer visible placement of beats. Students again are encouraged to use their imagination as they are audiating and to think of creative movements they may use to accompany the melody when they begin to move. A decrease in necessity of students imitating your movements should become increasingly evident.
4. Heretofore, emphasis has been placed on time (not musical time) and space in guiding students' movement. In translation of Rudolf Laban's usage, time is sustained or quick. Space is flexible (indirect) or direct. When sustained and flexible movements are combined, free-flowing continuous movement is a natural result. In contrast, when quick and direct movements are combined, movement becomes time-directed, suggesting a specific tempo. Two other words relating to movement are weight and flow, and both bear on musical expression and interpretation. Weight is light or strong. Flow is free or bound. For example, a march evokes strong and bound movement suggesting tension, whereas the blues elicit light and free movement prompting ease. All four effort motions in various combinations play a formidable role in elegant artistic movement.
5. Sixteenth notes are integral to each of the first three-patterns, each the length of an underlying dotted-quarter note. Weight and flow might reflect cascading positions of pairs of sixteenth notes as they combine differently with eighth notes.
6. The tie connecting measures 3 and 4 begins with a strong bound feeling superimposed on restrained free-flowing continuous movement into a diminuendo. That movement is contrasted with elongations in measures 5 and 6, the repetitious tonal

motive (B-natural to C) in association with a tie in measures 3 and 4, and an elongation in measure 5. The leading tone is stressed in terms of vigorous weight and withheld flow, but always in tandem with free-flowing continuous movement.

7. In measure 7, the eighth note progressing to the quarter note is undertaken with light free movement. After the rest in measure 8, which is an extension of (connected in motion to) the eighth-note/quarter-note pattern preceding it, anticipation of the eighth note to the quarter note is executed with strong bound movement. Dynamics and tempo are naturally expressed with weight and flow.
8. Indicated tonic, dominant-seventh, and subdominant chords, or alternate ones of your choosing in harmonic minor tonality, may be observed as you or a student accompany group singing using a chording instrument without marking macrobeats. Melody is always sung, not performed on an instrument.

Melody 5

Melody 5 is in harmonic minor tonality and usual triple meter. It is eight measures and includes tonic, dominant-seventh, and subdominant chords. Dotted-quarter notes = M.M. 56. C keyality may be transposed.

Pedagogy

1. Review Preparatory Relaxation Activities.
2. Again, students might be asked to audiate the melody before they begin to move, without you conducting or otherwise visually indicating beats. Students are encouraged to continue to render their imagination as they are audiating and to think of creative movements they may use to accompany the melody when they begin to move.
3. For all previous melodies, only upper parts of the body were moved. Now, for Melody 5, only lower parts of the body are moved. That includes hips, legs, knees, and feet. Although the torso may naturally move as lower parts of the body are moving, arms, hands, wrists, and fingers remain relatively motionless, and relaxation of the head, neck, and shoulders is sustained. Perhaps greatest benefit from moving lower parts of the body occurs when knees are rotated in the same direction or opposite directions. However, when rotated in the same direction, weight is maximized.
4. Sing the melody twice without a pause. Students are asked to begin moving in concert with the upbeat the second time the melody is begun. Students may move together, alternate as one group sings and another moves, or all students may sing as they are moving.
5. Upbeats to measures 1, 2, 5, and 6 flow into the melodic pattern they precede. The dotted-half note may move with a decrescendo, whereas the elongated dotted-quarter notes may move with a crescendo. After the upbeat pattern, the two thirty-second notes in measure 6 may be performed staccato with sustained crescendo.
6. It is an interesting phenomenon syncopation must be heard to be understood. To attempt to perform syncopation musically by reading notation without hearing it beforehand is unreasonable. Nevertheless, syncopation even unintentionally, takes on more a feeling of musical time than space and thus, apart from desired special effects, often tends to lack lengthiness. Durations are felt in the domain of space, whereas notes are read in the domain of musical time.

7. Measures 3 and 7 contain only syncopation. Weight and flow contribute to, facilitate, and solidify an artistic rendition of syncopation. Lower parts of the body are particularly suited for freely using weight. As hips move from side to side and/or in circular motion embracing weight, knees naturally shadow the action. Syncopation in conjunction with repeated pitches in measure 3 in comparison to syncopation in conjunction with downward melodic contour in measure 7 may be contrasted by sensitively moving lower body parts separately or together with bending or unbending knees.
8. All lower body parts may be engaged to provide assertive weight and resistant flow moving toward the B-natural in measure 5 and then gentle weight and free flow moving away from the B-natural in measure 7.
9. The elongation in the final measure merges with the upbeat pattern upon repetition of the melody without a pause in lower body movement.
10. Indicated tonic, dominant-seventh and subdominant chords, or alternate ones of your choosing in harmonic minor tonality, may be observed as you or a student accompany group singing using a chording instrument without marking macrobeats. Melody is always sung, not performed on an instrument.

Melody 6

Melody 6 is in major tonality, usual duple meter, and is eight measures. In addition to tonic, dominant-seventh, and subdominant chords, it includes tonic-seventh (C E G B♭), supertonic-seventh (D F♯ A C), submediant-seventh (A C♯ E G), and mediant-seventh (E G♯ B D) chords. Quarter notes = M.M. 72. Keyality may be transposed as desired.

Pedagogy

1. Review Preparatory Relaxation Activities.
2. Suggestions 2 and 3 for Melody 5 are apropos for Melody 6.
3. As with Melody 5, only lower parts of the body are moved.
4. Melody 6 begins with neither the tonic chord nor a pitch belonging to the tonic chord. In measure 5, tension continues with the tonic-seventh chord, and further, final resolution is delayed in measures 6 and 7 until two affirmative pitches of the tonic chord occur in measure 8. The rests in measures 6 and 8 also contribute to anticipation of an harmonic climax.
5. Because the same melodic pattern, except for one pitch, occurs in the first three-measures, the harmonic progression is of importance. When the chords are performed or audiated, they alleviate conceivable routine in the melody. Actuating dissonance between melody and harmony, which infuses interest into the repetitive pattern, provides a basis for creative body movement in relation to harmonic implications. In relation to harmonic structure, divergent physical movements may be marked indicating F♯ is an accented suspension in measures 1 and 2 but not in measure 3.
6. Simple movements may become more complex as the melody moves forward. Light and free movements may gradually become strong and bound. Circular rubato motion of knees agreeably reflect the duration of the half note in measure 4 in contrast to surrounding eighth notes.
7. The two rests are of particular significance. Each rest, belonging to the preceding pattern, creates an abrupt pause before the following pattern of eighth-notes is heard. Although there are pauses in the melody, there are no pause in movement. In fact, during the rests, anticipation of what is to be heard is artistically demonstrated with dynamic circular motion of the hips.

8. The same rhythm pattern supporting sequential pitches is present in measures 5 and 7. Rhythmic similarity but sequentially descending pitches offer an elegant opportunity to mirror melodic contour of the music. That may be accomplished by moving the same parts of the body in the same manner but other parts of the body differently when the two measures are performed.
9. The two eighth-notes in measures 6 and 8 request different motions. The first set suggests forward movement with a crescendo into measure 7, whereas the second set induces calm and closure as a result of a diminuendo and retardando reflected in the body.

Melody 7

Melody 7 is in harmonic minor tonality and usual duple meter. It is eight measures and includes the three common chords. Quarter notes = M.M. 90. As with preceding melodies, keyality may be transposed as desired. However, tessitura is maintained reasonably low so vocal force will not unwittingly detract from rhythmic thrust. A comparatively rapid tempo is recommended so rhythmic content may be accentuated.

Pedagogy

1. Review Preparatory Relaxation Activities.
2. Review suggestions 2 and 3 for Melody 5. Only lower parts of the body are moved.

3. Whereas Laban used concepts of time, space, weight, and flow to codify body movements, Jaques-Dalcroze combined weight and flow into a single concept of energy. Contradictory as it may seem, energy is greatest during rests. Rests embody movement and repose. Movement makes energy in space representative of feelings patently obvious.
4. Rests define the most influential characteristics of Melody 7. It was purposefully composed with emphasis on simplicity so as not to detract from the potency of rests propelling motion. Movements are made during eighth-note rests to anticipate and complement following note or notes. Specifically, except in measures 4 and 8, the intended chord is performed or audiated before pitches are sung. Various parts of the body accompanied by movements covering direct and flexible space are put into motion to contrast eighth-note rests preceding dotted-quarter notes to those preceding eighth notes. Rests provide underlying momentum as the melody gains in vitality from measure 1 through measure 4.
5. Rhythm pattern remains constant in measures 5, 6, and 7 as pitch contour becomes sequential in measures 5 and 6. Pitches rising in measure 7, beginning with the leading tone, move with abandon into measure 8 as the two thirty-second and eighth note pattern is rendered with eagerness.
6. Graceful and quieting movement in terms of fluency and lightness form the foundation for the quarter-note rest concluding the melody. Such movement compensates for a suspension of relaxation and closure as a result of the melody not ending on the tonic pitch. Moreover, anticipation is created by swift articulation of the two thirty-second note and eighth note pattern at the end.

Melody 8

Melody 8 is in major tonality and usual triple meter. It is eight measures and includes a variety of chords, including common progressions with a retrogression from the dominant-seventh to the mediant-seventh. Dotted-quarter notes = M.M. 76. Keyality may be transposed as desired.

Pedagogy

1. Review Preparatory Relaxation Activities.
2. Review suggestions 2 and 3 for Melody 5. Only lower parts of the body are moved.
3. The upbeat at the beginning of Melody 8 moves with a crescendo into measures 1 and 2. The body is reciprocal in this phrasing. The same is true for the upbeat in measure 2 moving into the phrase covering measures 3 and 4.
4. Shortness of sixteenth notes in measure 2 might be exaggerated with small rapid movements in knees and legs.
5. A diminuendo and retardando are integral to movement accompanying the half note in measure 4.
6. Measures 5 and 6 begin with non-scale tones stressed in body movement as measure 5 moves into measure 6 without a separate breath.
7. Pitches with accidentals in measures 5 and 6 are not dissonant. They are central to indicated chords. Thus, no special motion should be expended to call attention to their inordinate characteristics.
8. The sixteenth-note upbeats in measures 6 and 7 gain momentum with strong and bound effort motions.

9. It might be expected the chord following the dominant-seventh in measure 4 would be tonic. That being the case, the unpredicted mediant-seventh chord serves as a surprise. Free-flowing continuous movement of hips, legs, and knees add impetus to the one long phrase covering the final four measures. That phrase includes a common harmonic progression.
10. The melody does not end on the tonic pitch. Thus, because the measure is incomplete to coincide with the upbeat at the beginning of the melody, the final pitch can move gently into the upbeat. Though there may not be sufficient support using one deep breath to sing the final phrase of four measures continuing into the upbeat, that interpretation can be supplemented by manifesting free-flowing continuous movement using all lower parts of the body in parallel movements.

Melody 9

Melody 9 in harmonic minor tonality and usual combined meter is eight measures and includes typical chord progressions. Quarter notes = M.M. 70. Usual combined meter comprises both usual duple and triple rhythm patterns. Keyality may be transposed as desired.

Pedagogy

1. Review Preparatory Relaxation Activities.
2. Review suggestion 2 for Melody 5.

3. In previous melodies, upper and lower parts of the body were moved separately. Now, for Melody 9 and all melodies following, upper and lower parts of the body may be moved together. However, movements of upper and lower parts of the body are moved independently whenever desired. How upper and lower parts of the body are moved independently in association with deep breathing has heretofore been described.
4. Regardless of how the body is moved, stationary placement is maintained. That is, students do not move around the room. Their feet are firmly placed and legs are comfortably spread so the entire body ensures a center of weight and balance.
5. When moving the entire body, arms and hips tend to complement one another in circular motion. As a natural result, legs and knees move sympathetically. Hands and fingers are used to accentuate parts of the melody that might be otherwise less salient. All the while, free-flowing continuous movement is maintained without suggestion of musical time.
6. Melody 9 includes ties and rests. However, most compelling is the inclusion of triplets. The first triplet occurs in measure 2. Entire body movement is used to contrast the feeling of that triple pattern with duple patterns in measure 1. The same or different movements may be used to perform the triplet in measure 4. Whatever movements are used for those two triplets, they will naturally be different from those used with the triplet in measure 8. That is because the final triplet is approached with a tie.
7. Strong and bound movement seem best suited to the first two triplets, whereas light and free movement might reflect the triplet with a tie as it is released in cadential fashion, possibly with a retardando and diminuendo, toward the end of the melody. Movement in the last two measures underscores one deep breath underlying the entire phrase. Arms alone may well express a crescendo from the tied eighth-note to the following eighth notes in the final measure.
8. The sixteenth-note patterns following rests in measures 5 and 6 are anticipated with tension released suggesting a diminuendo

on the quarter note in measure 6. Wrists and fingers comfortably gesture artistic expression.

Melody 10

Melody 10 is in harmonic minor tonality, unusual meter, and is nine measures. It is in unusual meter because not all macrobeats are of equal temporal length. Dotted-quarter note macrobeats are shorter than the underlying dotted-half note macrobeats in measures 2 and 4, each comprising three quarter-note microbeats. Only tonic, dominant-seventh, and subdominant chords are used. Dotted-quarter notes = M.M. 78. Keyality may be transposed as desired.

Pedagogy

1. Review Preparatory Relaxation Activities.
2. Review suggestion 2 for Melody 5.
3. As with Melody 9, in Melody 10 upper and lower parts of the body may be moved together or independently .
4. A review of suggestions 4 and 5 for Melody 9 may prove helpful.
5. Whereas triplets were found in Melody 9, what is usually referred to as hemiola is an integral part of Melody 10. It fills measures 2 and 4. In common practice, it is said when three quarter-notes in one measure alternate with two groups of three eighth-notes in another measure, meter changes from compound duple to simple triple meter. Calling upon simple and compound to clarify the provision confuses the distinction.

The three eighth-notes are in usual triple meter as are the three quarter-notes. Simply, a temporal modulation takes place. Tempo is slower for three quarter-notes. That is, two macrobeats underlie two groups of three eighth-notes but only one longer macrobeat underlies one group of three quarter-notes.

6. The change of tempo within a constant meter is evidenced with contrasting movement of upper and lower parts of the body. Eighth notes exhibit powerful but restrained movement, whereas quarter notes are emblematic of feathery and released movement. Both types of movement emulate the work of choreographers that accurately contrasts the interaction of tempos. The entire body is called upon to respond to the quarter notes.
7. Beginning in measure 5, there is a sequence of cascading tied patterns culminating in a dotted-half note, requiring an extra measure that may be interpreted as a coda. With a deep breath and movement, especially with hips twisting in circular motion, the final five measures are performed as one phrase. Slight emphasis is placed on each eighth-note following a tie, but there is no suggestion of underlying macrobeats. Such action would instigate a sense of musical time.

Melody 11

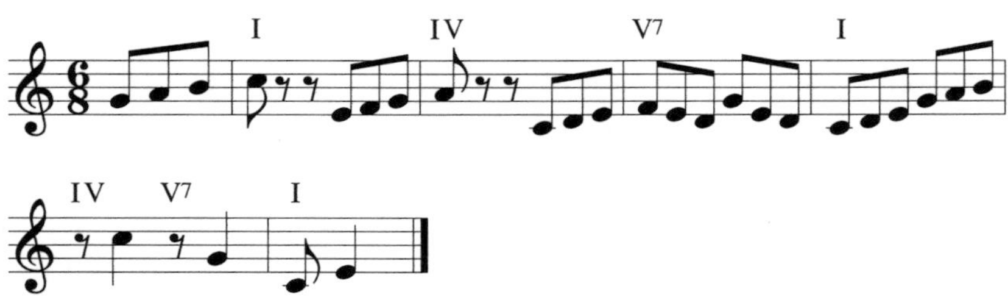

Melody 11 is in major tonality and usual triple meter. It is six measures and includes tonic, dominant-seventh, and subdominant chords. Dotted-quarter notes = M.M. 90. Keyality may be transposed as desired.

Pedagogy

1. Review Preparatory Relaxation Activities.
2. Review suggestion 3 for Melody 3.
3. Upper and lower parts of the body are moved together. However, beginning with Melody 11, students take full advantage of space by engaging in locomotion as they move around the room. Remaining in place moving upper and/or lower parts of the body is nonlocomotive. Traveling around the room moving upper and/or lower parts of the body is locomotive. Students move freely around the room, perhaps even making 180 degree turns, as they mobilize upper, lower, or both domains of the body simultaneously in free-flowing continuous movement. The Latin loco means from a place.
4. Ability to move three-dimensionally (upper and lower body in locomotion) when traveling around the room is comfortably acquired when sequential transition is made from two-dimensional (upper and lower body in nonlocomotion) while remaining in place, as exemplified in suggestions accompanying the previous ten melodies.
5. Model locomotive space synchronized with upper and lower body movement in league with deep breathing. The model does not include or even suggest keeping time by pausing between macrobeats or accenting macrobeats. Meter is felt but not seen. Movements do not include conducting, and in no way do they indicate stylized or otherwise memorized steps for folk dancing. If anything, ballet motion is the rule, no reference being made to counting beats or musical time.
6. When moving three-dimensionally, during locomotion, shoes are removed and stocking feet are not lifted from the floor. Feet slide along the floor. A smooth wooden floor is advocated for this activity. If feet are lifted in locomotion, they are naturally raised and placed as if walking, dancing, or marching. Thus, macrobeats and microbeats become obvious, and space undesirably supercedes musical time.
7. It is important when students move around the room either one or more upper or lower parts of the body are in constant motion.

Preferably, parts of both the upper and lower body are moving at all times as the body is traveling in an uncluttered environment.

8. Sing the melody twice without a pause. Students are asked to begin moving in concert with the upbeat the second time the melody is begun. That the melody does not end on the tonic pitch contributes to fluidity of flowing movement into the upbeat upon repetition of the melody.
9. Gliding in light and free continuous space may reflect the one phrase covering the second part of measure 2 through measure 4 with the rest thrusting strong and bound agogic anticipation of measure five. The melody is purposely short to provide for physically demonstrating the sustained phrase. The eighth note in measure 6 is fulfillment of eighth-note rests in measure 5.

Melody 12

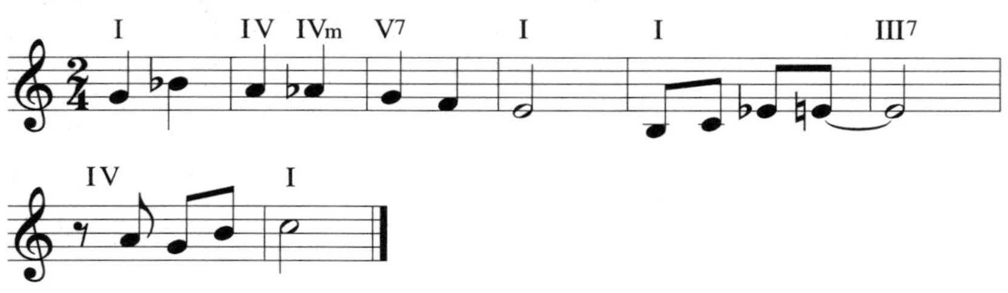

Melody 12 is in major tonality and usual duple meter. It is eight measures and includes subdominant minor and mediant-seventh chords. Quarter notes = M.M. 100. Keyality may be transposed as desired.

Pedagogy

1. Review Preparatory Relaxation Activities.
2. Review suggestion 2 for Melody 5.
3. Upper and lower parts of the body are moved together. Suggestions 4 and 5 for Melody 9 may be reviewed. As with Melody 11, students take full advantage of space by engaging in locomotion as they move the entire body. That is, they move

freely around the room, perhaps even making 180 degree turns, as they mobilize upper, lower, or both domains of the body simultaneously in free-flowing continuous locomotive movement.

4. Model locomotive space synchronized with upper and lower body movement in league with deep breathing. The model does not include or even suggest keeping time by pausing between macrobeats or accenting macrobeats. Meter is felt but not seen. Movements do not include conducting, and in no way do they indicate stylized or otherwise memorized steps for folk dancing. If anything, ballet motion is the rule, no reference at all being made to counting beats or musical time.
5. When moving three-dimensionally, in locomotion, shoes are removed and stocking feet are not lifted from the floor. Feet slide along the floor. A smooth wooden floor is recommended for this activity. If feet are lifted during locomotion, they are naturally raised and placed as if walking, dancing, or marching. Thus, macrobeats and microbeats become obvious and space undesirably supercedes musical time.
6. Also important when students move around the room is either one or more upper or lower parts of the body are in constant motion. Preferably, parts of both the upper and lower body are moving at all times as the body is traveling in uncluttered space.
7. Chromaticism is a distinguishing characteristic of Melody 12. In particular, light and free movement is well suited to serve as accompaniment throughout the sweeping descending line at the beginning. With deep breathing, light and free movement is sustained as the contrasting ascending line with shorter durations is performed beginning in measure 5. The melody offers an opportunity to use opposing movements in the upper and lower body, as pace of locomotion is sustained to highlight divergent direction and speed in the melody.
8. The subdominant-minor chord in measure 2 in conjunction with chromaticism in the melody may be made particularly poignant using complementary body movements.

9. Though there is a rest in measure 7, movement is continued during silence. The three-notes in measures 7 are robust and controlled, but the half note in measure 8 reinstates a feeling of fine touch and release.
10. Acknowledgement is made obvious, perhaps with head and facial features, as the chord but not the pitch of the melody changes from measure 5 to measure 6. Arms might relate to the pitch, whereas hips might accentuate changed harmony.

Melody 13

Melody 13 is in Dorian tonality, C keyality, and usual duple meter. It is eight measures and includes subtonic chords. Quarter notes = M.M. 85. Notice the harmonic progression includes subtonic chords in measures 2 and 6, which is the equivalent of the dominant-seventh chord in major tonality. Also, although tonic (I) is a minor chord, subtonic (VII) and subdominant (IV) are major chords.

Pedagogy

1. A review of Preparatory Relaxation Activities and suggestions 3 through 7 for Melody 11 may be helpful. Keep in mind suggestion 2 for Melody 5. Remember, remaining in place moving upper and/or lower parts of the body is called nonlocomotive space. Traveling around the room moving upper and/or lower parts of the body is called locomotive space.

2. Movement in nonlocomotive space and locomotive space may be alternated upon repetitions of Melody 13. Alternation of nonlocomotive and locomotive space is infrequent within one rendition of the melody.
3. Free-flowing continuous movement is maintained throughout the melody. Though in measure 2 the two sixteenth-notes noticeably contrast preceding quarter notes in the flow of the melody, they are not pointed or assertive. They are simply acknowledged in gentle and buoyant movement using small muscles in the upper part of the body. Delicate finger movement would be fitting.
4. As with the sixteenth notes, the body moves through the rest in the final measure with unrestricted grace and freedom. Using upper and lower body parts in nonlocomotive and locomotive space, carefree movement is directed toward a decrescendo and retardando.
5. One deep breath, mirrored in leisurely movement, connects measures 4 and 5. Similarly, breathing is unbroken between measures 6 and 7. In both cases, using forceful and controlled movement, there is a suggestion of crescendo throughout the duration of the half note and tied eighth-note culminating in a subito piano when the second eighth-note in measure 7 is sounded.
6. Characteristic tones in Dorian tonality, as compared to harmonic minor tonality, are the raised sixth step (A in measure 3) and lowered seventh step (B♭ in measures 6 and 7). Rarified movement highlights those pitches. Upward head motion is common when A is performed. Downward head and arm motion is normal when B♭ is performed. In singing, A is rendered slightly higher and B♭ slightly lower in terms of equal temperament.

Melody 14

Melody 14 is in Mixolydian tonality, C keyality, and usual triple meter. It is eight measures and includes subtonic chords. Dotted-quarter notes = M.M. 92. There are only two chords in the melody. One is subtonic, which is equivalent to the dominant-seventh in major tonality.

Pedagogy

1. A review of Preparatory Relaxation Activities and suggestions 3 through 7 for Melody 11 may be helpful. Keep in mind suggestion 2 for Melody 5. As with Melody 13, upper and lower parts of the body are activated as students engage in movement in nonlocomotive space and locomotive space in accompaniment to Melody 14.
2. Movement in nonlocomotive space and locomotive space may be alternated upon repetitions of Melody 14. Alternation of nonlocomotive and locomotive space is infrequent within one rendition of the melody.
3. Mixolydian tonality, when compared to major tonality, has one characteristic tone. It is the lowered seventh step. B♭ occurs in the upbeat pattern. Being the first pitch of the melody, it is performed using strong and bound movement with a gradual decrescendo to the elongation in measure 6. The second group of three eighth-notes in measure 7 is articulated with vigorous and restrained staccato movement in the lower part of the body, preferably using hips and knees. When moving in locomotive space, an abrupt stop in place may be enacted while the entire body is engaged in free-flowing continuous movement.

4. The subtonic pitch occurs five times and the subtonic chord twice throughout the melody. However, only once do they coincide in measure 7. The distinction is noted as the body floats.
5. After you sing the melody, without a pause students are instructed to begin moving in concert with the upbeat when the melody begins again.
6. Upbeats are prevalent throughout the melody. They share similar movements using the same parts of the upper body but dissimilar movements using the same parts of the lower body, or vice versa. The divergent movements are consistent with contrasting melodic contours.
7. Given upbeats in conjunction with elongations in measures 1 and 2, melodic flow in measure 3 is a surprise. The same is true for measures 4, 5, and 6 moving to measure 7. It is expected the motif will carry forth. This thwarted expectation is duly noted as movements in measures 1 and 2 are contrasted with those in measure 3, and movements in measures 4, 5, and 6 are contrasted with those in measure 7. Movements in measures 3 and 7 may counterbalance one another.
8. The six elongations in the melody include only tonic and dominant pitches. In addition to other expressive movements, the same motions might be used each time one or the other pitch is heard.

Melody 15

Melody 15 is in harmonic minor tonality and unusual paired meter. It is eight measures, and because of unusual meter, the harmonic progression is straightforward. Eighth notes = M.M. 160. In usual meter, macrobeats are of equal temporal length. That is true for usual duple, usual triple, and usual combined meters. In unusual meter, all macrobeats are not of equal temporal length but microbeats are of equal temporal length. For example, in 5/8 some macrobeats may be quarter notes (groupings of two eighth-notes) and others dotted-quarter notes (groupings of three eighth-notes). All eighth notes are microbeats. Unusual meter is paired when there are two underlying macrobeats in a rhythm pattern (filling one complete measure in 5/8) and unpaired when there are three underlying macrobeats in a rhythm pattern (filling one complete measure in 7/8, as in Melody 16).

Pedagogy

1. If necessary, review Preparatory Relaxation Activities and suggestions 3 through 7 for Melody 11. Keep in mind suggestion 2 for Melody 5. As with Melody 14, upper and lower parts of the body are activated as students move in nonlocomotive space and locomotive space in accompaniment to Melody 15.
2. Movement in nonlocomotive space and locomotive space may be alternated upon repetitions of Melody 15. Alternation of nonlocomotive and locomotive space is infrequent within one rendition of the melody.
3. It is imperative macrobeats not be marked with feet while moving around the room. If that appears to be arduous initially, students may remain in place as the body is engaged in free-flowing continuous movement throughout each measure, especially using hips and legs, without accentuating macrobeats or microbeats. With that achieved, students may gradually begin moving around the room again without offering a hint of marching.
4. The first four measures of Melody 15 have the same sequence of underlying microbeats. That is, microbeats are audiated in groups of twos followed by groups of threes. Measures 5 and 6 are reversed. Microbeat groupings in measures 7 and 8 represent

a recapitulation. Alternating the sequence of macrobeats is epitomized with body movements.

5. Measures 2, 4, and 8 include undivided macrobeats, and measure 8 includes divisions of microbeats (sixteenth notes). These differences may be modeled with counterbalanced movements of wrists, fingers, and elbows in terms of weight and flow. Use of linear and elastic space is of special significance in this exposition.

Melody 16

Melody 16 is major tonality and unusual unpaired meter. It is eight measures and includes tonic, dominant-seventh, and subdominant chords. Eighth notes = M.M. 160.

Pedagogy

1. As with Melody 15, upper and lower parts of the body are activated as students move in nonlocomotive space and locomotive space in accompaniment to Melody 16.
2. Movement in nonlocomotive space and locomotive space may be alternated upon repetitions of Melody 16. Alternation of nonlocomotive and locomotive space is infrequent within one rendition of the melody.
3. It is imperative macrobeats not be marked with feet while moving around the room. If that appears to be arduous initially, students may remain in place as the body is engaged in free-flowing

continuous movement throughout each measure, especially using hips and legs, without accentuating macrobeats or microbeats. With that achieved, students may gradually begin moving around the room again without offering a hint of marching.

4. Although Melody 16 is eight measures, it comprises more notes than Melody 15. The primary reason is there are three underlying macrobeats in rhythm patterns. Thus, a sequence of underlying macrobeats remains consistent throughout the melody. Two underlying macrobeats are always followed by three underlying macrobeats.
5. There are two and three chord changes within patterns (measures). In polarity, pitches within a group for the most part are repetitious. Simplicity of the melody in comparison to harmonic changes is idiosyncratic in Melody 16. Perhaps upper parts of the body may focus on melodic content and lower parts on harmonic progressions, or the entire body may centralize melodic content. Moving in locomotive space may acknowledge strong and direct abruptness contrasted with light and indirect flow to coincide with harmonic implications.
6. Melody 16 is cohesive in form. Measures 1 through 4 may be considered part A, measures 5 and 6 part B, and measures 7 and 8 a paraphrased partial recapitulation of measures 1 and 2.
7. The final rhythm pattern in measure 8 is unique. It embraces only macrobeats. While announcing finality of the melody, movement may represent the epitome of light, free, and indirect motion while the body remains in gentle repose.

Melody 17

Melody 17 is in harmonic minor tonality and usual triple meter. It is eight measures and includes tonic, dominant-seventh, and subdominant chords. Dotted-quarter notes = M.M. 76.

Pedagogy

1. As before, upper and lower parts of the body are in motion in nonlocomotive space and locomotive space. Moreover, when moving to previous melodies, some students sang as they or others engaged in physical activities, they or you performed an harmonic accompaniment as indicated by chord symbols using a chording instrument, or they provided an harmonic accompaniment by incidentally singing chords, an obbligato, an ostinato, chord roots, thirds and sixths, and so on. So as not to detract from appropriate movement, special suggestions were not given previously for harmonic accompaniments. However, now while you and students continue to sing the melody and move, chords are appropriately sung in a specified manner. A minimum of three students (or you and two students) is necessary to perform these chords.
2. Chord voicings for Melody 17 in harmonic minor tonality and Melody 18 in major tonality are notated below. Also, in the event it is desired to sing chords for Melody 13 in Dorian tonality and Melody 14 in Mixolydian tonality, appropriate chords are also notated below. The preferred chord voicing contributes to and enhances vocal improvisation and creative movement when performed legato, not marking macrobeats.

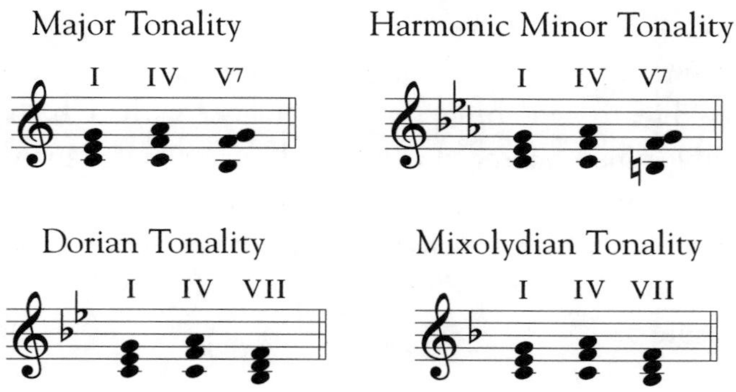

3. As explained, whereas to create means to relate and the root meaning of art is to fit together, the root meaning of improvisation is not provided or not foreseen. Occasional periods of vocal silence and physical stillness (no movement at all) in performance play a stunning role in improvisation.
4. Students individually may improvise a melody based on the notated chord progression for Melody 17 as a group of three persons collectively perform the chord progression. Or, individual students in one group may simultaneously improvise melodies as another group performs the chord progression and still another group moves. Harmonic improvisations are inspiring, quite different from simple variations of a melody.
5. It is expected as chord progressions are heard and improvisation is taking place, an individual or group of students will take turns engaging in creative movement. Creative movement in locomotive space is effortlessly a natural concomitant of improvisation, even more so when body-creativity corresponds to vocal improvisation.
6. Of course, when improvisation is undertaken, suggestions for accompanied creative movement may only be conjectured. Nonetheless, to the extent rhythmic characteristics of the notated melody are retained, the following suggestions may prove helpful.
7. The eighth-note groupings in measures 1 and 3 are interpreted as robust and bound, and during the rest, airy and streaming-out roundabout space provides a compelling contrast. Free-flowing continuous movement might be smoothly phased into measures 2 and 4.
8. Measures 5 through 7 might be sustained as one phrase, a deep breath matching the movement, with a bold staccato ending superimposed on the final eighth notes in measure 8. The octave skip in measure 8 is acknowledged, particularly in association with its melodic downward direction in opposition to melodic upward direction of the diminished-seventh in measure 5.

Melody 18

Melody 18 is in major tonality and usual duple meter. It is eight measures and includes supertonic-seventh and submediant-seventh chords. Quarter notes = M.M. 84. Chord voicing for major tonality is found under suggestion 3 for Melody 17.

Pedagogy

1. Review suggestions 4 through 7 for Melody 17 for recommendations concerning improvisation and creative movement. If not already incorporated into improvisation with Melody 17, the use of non-harmonic (non-chord) pitches might be used with Melody 18. Combining chord pitches with non-chord pitches provides for fluid improvisation.
2. As before, upper and lower parts of the body are in motion as students move in locomotive space. Regardless of structure of improvisation, though always taken into consideration, creative movement may be enriched and made more enjoyable and challenging by pairs of students cooperating in movement. For example, one student may initiate movement with a one or more parts of the upper or lower body while the other mirrors exact movement. Or, the second student might offer a creative response to movement by engaging in immediate or delayed opposite motions and/or using contrary upper or lower area of the body. Similarly, movements may be rendered by one pair of students in response to another pair.

3. Particularly venturous movement occurs when one member of a pair remains in nonlocomotive space while the other moves in locomotive space. Movement may take place directly or indirectly on repetitions of Melody 18, and students may exchange positions and use varying combinations of strong, light, bound, and free effort motions as they are ambulatory.
4. Following ideas in suggestion 3, one or more students may move body parts while in a sitting or lying position while others remain standing as they are moving cooperatively or otherwise.
5. In measures 1 and 2, slurs are combined with elongations. Upper parts of the body, especially arms, hands, and fingers, may confirm slurs. Lower parts of the body, especially hips and knees, may sustain elongations.
6. In contrast to slurred elongations, ties connect measures 3 and 4 and measures 7 and 8. The difference between elongations and ties may be exaggerated gracefully in movement.
7. The dotted-eighth and sixteenth-note patterns in the first two measures may be overstated to set the character of the melody. That may be accomplished by an almost imperceptible bound separation of the longer duration from the shorter one, and an exaggeration of a suggested extension of the longer duration.
8. The harmonic progression naturally evolving from measure 5 and resolving in measure 8 offers an excellent opportunity to reflect free-flowing continuous movement. Within that phrase, a body-crescendo to a staid rest in measure 7 is made prominent. After a startling body pause in association with the rest, it is contrasted with a rubato body-decrescendo in the final two measures.

Melody 19

Melody 19 is in major tonality and usual triple meter. It is twelve measures incorporating common chord progressions. Dotted-quarter notes = M.M. 88.

Pedagogy

1. With previous melodies, both upper and lower parts of the body were in motion as students moved in locomotive space. However, now that students are agile in and confident about exploring space apart from time, superimposing musical time on space in movement initially in nonlocomotive space is introduced in Melody 19. It is accomplished by flicking wrists while upper parts of the body, particularly arms, are in graceful free-flowing continuous movement. Clapping is conspicuously avoided. It is imperative students initially remain nonlocomotive. Only later, when developing advanced physical coordination, will musical time be marked by using both upper and lower parts of the body in nonlocomotive space. Also at that time walking, marching, and dancing in locomotive space may be undertaken in association with flicking wrists and sweeping arms.
2. The purpose of flicking wrists on macrobeats as arms are continuously and freely moving is to audiate space. The physical distance in space between flicking wrists, one macrobeat after another, soon may be transferred to measured space in audiation. That is, with sufficient capability, audiation of the actual feeling of spatial distance between flicks renders

prescribed physical movements unnecessary. Accurate placement of macrobeats is concomitant with consistent tempo that neither rushes nor slows.

3. As will be explained in association with the final four-melodies, combining continuous free-flowing movement with macrobeats and microbeats indications gives evidence of musical time. Macrobeats establish tempo in both usual and unusual meters. How macrobeats of equal temporal length are divided into microbeats establishes usual meter. How macrobeats of unequal temporal lengths are grouped establishes unusual meter. Tempo and meter are the essentials of musical time.
4. After Melody 19 becomes familiar to students, while remaining in nonlocomotive space, you model flicking both wrists to coincide with macrobeats (dotted-quarter notes). Soon, a small group of students sing the melody as other students move and flick their wrists to macrobeats in nonlocomotive space. After they are able to flick wrists in the described manner, engaging in locomotive space is permissible. However, when moving in locomotive space, feet do not leave the floor. Students slide or glide on their feet. Students may find it helpful if you unobtrusively chant *bah* on consecutive macrobeats.
5. Because Melody 19 is twelve measures it provides ample opportunity for developing consistency of tempo in protracted movement. Its abbreviated ABA form may be made obvious with complimentary motions.
6. Style and expression are easily achieved as wrists are in flicking motion. For example, eighth notes occurring on macrobeats in elongation patterns may be concurrent with flicks. Nonetheless, they need not be exaggerated. They flow gently and are dispensed with quickness and diminution. Also, during dotted-half notes, hips and knees naturally form a flowing foundation for the punctuation of wrist movement.

Melody 20

Melody 20 is in harmonic minor tonality and usual duple meter. It is eight measures and includes an expected harmonic progression. Quarter notes = M.M. 80.

Pedagogy

1. As before, upper parts of the body are in flicking motion as students remain in nonlocomotive space or move in locomotive space to Melody 20. However, now that students are confident in flicking macrobeats (quarter notes), they may also begin to creatively attend to microbeats (eighth notes). Hips and knees may mark macrobeats or wrist and finger movements may coincide with microbeats. (Movement to macrobeats and microbeats simultaneously is postponed until Melodies 21 and 22 are introduced.)
2. A review of suggestions 2 and 3 for Melody 19 is recommended.
3. After Melody 20 becomes familiar to students, you remain in nonlocomotive space modeling flicking wrists while moving fingers of both hands to coincide with microbeats as movement of hips and knees coincides with macrobeats. Soon, a small group of students sing the melody as others move to microbeats and macrobeats. After they are able to flick wrists and move fingers in the described manner, moving hips and knees and legs and feet to macrobeats in locomotive space is permissible. However, when moving in locomotive space, feet do not leave the floor. Students slide or glide on their feet. Students may

find it helpful if you unobtrusively chant bah on consecutive macrobeats.

4. Dotted-quarter and half notes in Melody 20 are sustained with free-flowing continuous movement, giving no evidence of tension, as the second macrobeat embodied in dotted-quarter notes is marked with pointed movement using lower parts of the body. Although various parts of the body are responding to different concerns, movements complement one another.
5. Macrobeats and microbeats occur within sixteenth-note groupings. Corresponding movements of both types of beats are recognized and may be complementary or oppositional as singing of the melody cautiously articulates quickness of the sixteenth-notes.
6. Tonal and rhythm content of measures 5 and 6 is sequential to measures 3 and 4. That may be made poignant using the same parts of the body with slightly different extensions of movements, all the while placement of macrobeats and microbeats is clearly evident.
7. Exceptional characteristics of Melody 20 may be pronounced in unique movement. The harmonic progression begins with a dominant-seventh chord, the melody does not end on the tonic pitch, and the raised seventh step (B-natural), the leading tone, is not embedded in the melody. Divergent movement may be undertaken within one performance or upon repetitions of the melody to exemplify its relatively exceptional attributes.

Melody 21

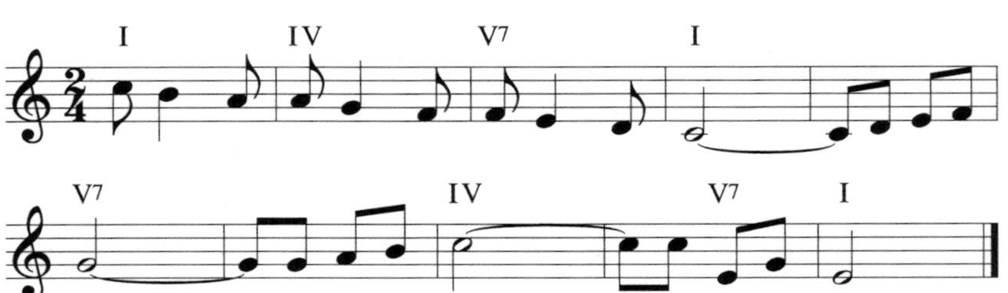

Melody 21 is in major tonality and usual duple meter. It is ten measures including a common harmonic progression. Quarter notes = M.M. 96.

Pedagogy

1. It may have been discovered some students are unable to move parts of their body to microbeats while at the same time moving other parts to macrobeats. That is evidence of lack of physical coordination. As moving in nonlocomotive space is readiness for coordination, coordination is readiness for moving to macrobeats and microbeats simultaneously.
2. To assist students in becoming physically coordinated, the following sequential procedure is recommended. Use of body weight is of extraordinary importance in the process. Students are not singled out and worked with individually. The class as a whole participates in the activity. The procedure is repeated at the beginning of each period until the majority of students demonstrate self reliance in physically moving to macrobeats and microbeats simultaneously.
3. Model each of the following eleven steps one at a time and asks students to watch and imitate each action. As soon as most students show proficiency with a step, a segue takes place into the next step (each step moving into the other without a pause). Going from the first to the final step should not take more than ten minutes.
   - Sitting and leaning slightly forward, both elbows rest on top of the desk and forearms together move up and down in the same direction. Because use of weight is necessary, wrists and fingers remain firm and do not move independently of the forearm.
   - Sitting and leaning slightly forward with both elbows resting on top of the desk, forearms alternately move up and down. Again, wrists and fingers remain firm and they do not move independently of the forearm.
   - Sitting, heels of both feet together move up and down in the same direction. Toes are not tapped because toe tapping lacks weight and creates muscle tension.

- Sitting, heels of both feet alternately move up and down.
- Sitting, the body sways from side to side, shifting weight from one hip to the other. Use of weight is maximized with this action. Rocking back and forth lacks weight.
- Standing, both arms swing together back and forth in the same direction. Arms do not move in different directions.
- Sitting and leaning slightly forward, both elbows rest on top of the desk and forearms together move up and down in the same direction. At the same time, heels of both feet together move up and down in the same direction. That is, both arms and both feet are moving simultaneously.
- Standing, the body is rocked from side to side, one leg to the other. Legs may be lifted or the body twisted as knees bend.
- Standing, the body is rocked from side to side, one leg to the other. At the same time, both arms from the shoulder are quietly slapped against thighs. Neither wrist nor finger movement may be substituted for the weight of full arm movement. Both legs and both arms perform macrobeats.
- Standing, the body is rocked from side to side, one leg to the other. At the same time, both arms from the shoulder are quietly slapped against thighs. However, now only legs are performing macrobeats. Arms are performing usual duple meter microbeats. That is, in 2/4, legs are moving to quarter notes and arms are simultaneously moving to eighth notes.
- Sitting and leaning slightly forward, both elbows rest on top of the desk and forearms together move up and down in the same direction to duple meter microbeats as heels of both feet together move up and down in the same direction to macrobeats. At this point students have acquired sufficient coordination to audiate and physically perform macrobeats and duple meter microbeats simultaneously. They have reached the goal. It is necessary to start at the beginning and, with one exception, follow each of the eleven sequential steps to coordinate students in usual triple meter. In the final step, in 6/8, legs are moving to dotted-quarter notes and arms are moving to eighth notes.

4. As an individual student or a group of students are engaging in free-flowing continuous movement in nonlocomotive space or locomotive space, remaining students are performing Melody 21 with or without harmonic accompaniment while moving arms to duple microbeats and legs to macrobeats. Students take turns engaging in different activities.
5. If students tend to move their arms in synchrony with syncopation of the melody rather than to microbeats, it may be determined they are not yet satisfactorily coordinated and work further with the eleven steps is necessary. Or, if students tend not to perform individual macrobeats during half notes tied to eighth notes, remedial or compensatory instruction pertaining to coordination readiness is essential.
6. Once you believe students are consciously audiating with accuracy, it is suggested they unconsciously (not preplanned) display macrobeats and duple microbeats with creative physical movements. That is, precise prescribed physical movements are replaced by creative body movements intimating, but not accenting macrobeats and microbeats, without sacrificing free-flowing continuous movement. Macrobeats and microbeats may be manifested with any part of the body at any time. The objective is movement with musical expression demonstrated primarily by using head, neck, shoulders, arms, hands, and fingers. Creative movements of lower parts of the body, though not as obvious, support and complement movements above the waist.
7. Creative movement may underscore the melodic sequences in measures 1 through 3 and measures 4 through 9. The final two measures serve as a coda. That the melody does not end on the tonic pitch may be featured by, upon repetition, phasing it with a deep breath into the beginning pitch of the melody.

Melody 22

Melody 22 is in harmonic minor tonality and usual triple meter. It is eight measures and includes common chords. Dotted-quarter notes = M.M. 56.

Pedagogy

1. Development of coordination and guidance in moving lower parts of the body to macrobeats while moving upper parts of the body to microbeats has been explained in pedagogical suggestions for Melody 21. As soon as possible, prescribed movements to macrobeats and microbeats ceases, at least suspended until remedial or compensatory instruction may be necessary.
2. However, as explained, before students may be expected to respond to macrobeats and microbeats simultaneously in usual triple meter, all coordination steps are repeated with the following exception. In the eleventh step, both arms from the shoulder are quietly slapped against thighs with three microbeats rather than two in coordination with macrobeats. If students tend to use wrists and fingers in place of entire arms, the error is corrected immediately. The role and necessity of weight must be made clear, and a slower tempo may be requisite to achieve the goal.
3. Now, students are asked only to audiate macrobeats and microbeats as they perform and move to Melody 22. That is, they audiate macrobeats and microbeats appropriately without the accompanying aforementioned prescribed movements. Once you believe students are consciously audiating with accuracy, it is

suggested they unconsciously (not preplanned) display macrobeats and triple microbeats with creative physical movements. That is, precise prescribed physical movements are replaced by creative body movements that acknowledge, not accent, macrobeats and microbeats without sacrificing free-flowing continuous movement. Macrobeats and microbeats may be manifested with any part of the body at any time. The intent is movement with musical expression demonstrated primarily by using head, neck, shoulders, arms, hands, and fingers. Creative movements of lower parts of the body, though not as obvious, support and complement movements above the waist.

4. The slurred tie in measures 5 and 6 might be alluded to with concurrent notice of the underlying eighth-note microbeat and change of pitch. Similarly, agogic accents during the dotted-half note and rests with various movements may indicate the second macrobeat without physical stress.
5. A reversal of sixteenth and eighth notes sequences in patterns occurs in measure 3. Moving swiftly and without anxiety or doubt, placement of audiated, not physically demonstrated, macrobeats becomes obvious.
6. The rest in the final measure is highlighted using movement expressing surprise and possibly astonishment. Nonetheless, the final three-notes serve as an abrupt coda, as reflected in staccato movements.

Melody 23

Melody 23 is in major tonality and usual triple meter. It is eight measures and includes common chord progressions. Dotted-quarter notes = M.M. 74.

Pedagogy

1. With students having received guidance in accord with sequential suggestions associated with previous melodies, they have acquired sufficient macrobeat and microbeat readiness to perform and move rhythmically. Given those two underlying parts of rhythm, familiarity with the third fundamental part, rhythm patterns, forms a composite. With that knowledge, students participate in rhythm activities with competence and confidence. Rhythm solfege contributes effectively to that end. Any theoretical information students may lack is quickly supplemented using their broad music backgrounds and acquired practical capabilities as a foundation.
2. Melodic patterns comprise both tonal and rhythm elements, whereas tonal patterns, which are sung, include only pitches, and rhythm patterns, which are chanted, include only durations. Examples of rhythm patterns students are most frequently exposed to are notated below. Ten rhythm patterns in usual duple meter are followed by twelve rhythm patterns in usual triple meter.

Usual Duple Meter

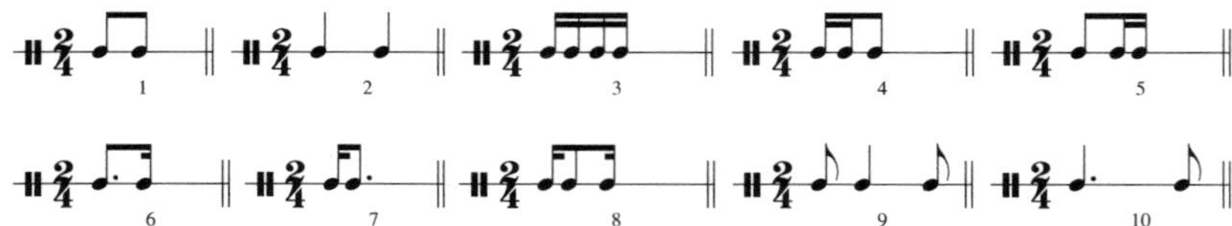

Usual Triple Meter

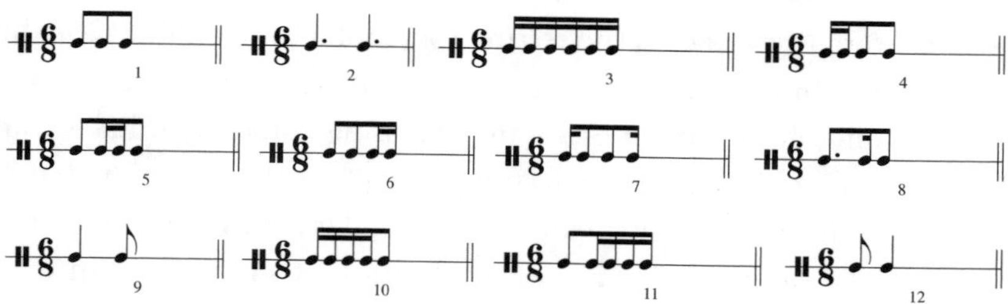

3. The illustrated rhythm syllables on page 53 are based on beat functions, not on time-value names of notes. A brief explanation of the preferred solfege follows. For an inclusive discussion of rhythm solfege and rhythm patterns, read my book, *Rhythm: Contrasting the Implications of Audiation and Notation*. It is listed in the Bibliography.
   - Different syllables are used for macrobeats and microbeats regardless of meter. Thus, patterns within a meter as well as patterns in different meters, including both usual and unusual, are distinguished by use of different syllables logically related and easily generalized. Numbers are not used.
   - Different syllables are used for successive microbeats in usual triple meter, depending on their placement in a pattern, not in a measure.
   - Regardless of meter in which they are found, macrobeats are always associated with the same syllable. Thus, macrobeats of different lengths in unusual meters, compared to usual meters, and those found within each unusual meter share the same syllable. Further, the same syllable is used for all macrobeats regardless of their placement in a measure. Thus, need for counting is eliminated and tempos remain stable and consistent. Because the same syllable is used for all macrobeats in a measure and a different syllable is used for each microbeat, with syllables for microbeats changing to indicate different meter, students are guided in distinguishing between macrobeats and microbeats in all meters and among meters

themselves. Just as students demonstrate their sense of tonality when they audiate *do* as the resting tone in major tonality and *la* as the resting tone in harmonic minor tonality, so they demonstrate a sense of meter when they audiate microbeats in different meters using different syllables and audiate microbeats with unique syllables in unusual meters. In addition, they distinguish length and groupings of macrobeats.

- The same syllable is used for division of a microbeat into two parts, regardless of meter and placement of divisions in the pattern or measure.
- In the case of an elongation, be it of a macrobeat, microbeat, or even a division of a microbeat, the same syllable is sustained throughout. Most important, it is sustained without imposing dynamic accents for consecutively connected macrobeats or microbeats.
- Syllables given to durations in a pattern are also audiated (chanted silently) for rests corresponding to beats and divisions of beats. Therefore, rests naturally become a functional part of the pattern they precede, follow, or both.
- Syllables used for complete patterns are also used for upbeat patterns, each phrased in association with the first macrobeat of the complete pattern it precedes.

4. Determination of specific rhythm patterns in a melody is subjective. You and students may have differing opinions, and that is not only to be expected, but also to be encouraged. After each set of inferences is acknowledged, rhythm patterns are performed using rhythm syllables.
5. Then, as the entire melody is chanted in tempo using rhythm syllables (all on the same pitch but with musical nuance) by one group of students, another group is pursuing free-flowing creative movement. Upon melodic repetitions, groups change activities.
6. In both chanting and movement, there are no accents on macrobeats, nor is duration of the dotted-half note punctuated to indicate placement of the second macrobeat. Moreover, a crescendo is not made to macrobeats following an elongation or tie.

Usual Duple Meter

Usual Triple Meter

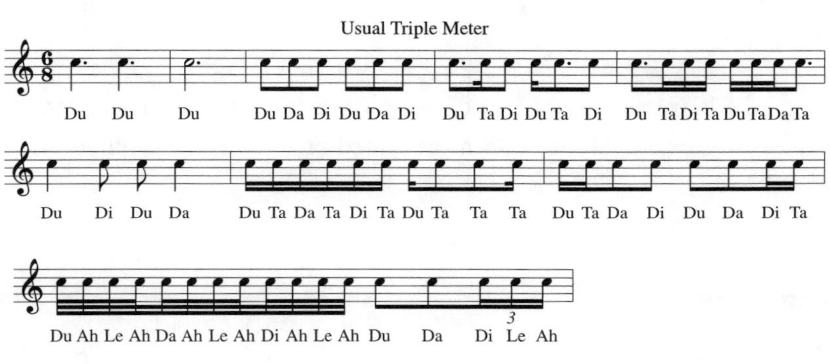

Usual Combined Meter

Unusual Paired Meter

Unusual Unpaired Meter

Melody 24

Melody 24 is in harmonic minor tonality and usual duple meter. It is ten measures and includes common chord progressions. Quarter notes = M. M. 80.

Pedagogy

1. Review suggestions 1, 2, and 3 for Melody 23. Remember, although macrobeats and microbeats are not accented in singing, chanting, or moving, they are continually audiated with or without accents. Unless for special effects, a crescendo is not made to macrobeats.
2. In measure 3, the first macrobeat sixteenth-note is approached with a tie and harmonic change. That alone sufficiently suggests placement of the macrobeat in a musical manner.
3. Rhythm patterns are performed using rhythm syllables. Then, as the entire melody is chanted in tempo using rhythm syllables (all on the same pitch but with musical nuance) by one group of students, another group is pursuing free-flowing creative movement. Upon repetitions of the melody, groups change activities.
4. You sing the melody twice without a pause. Students are instructed to begin moving in concert with the upbeat the second time the melody is begun. However, no accent is made on the macrobeat following the upbeat. The final dotted-quarter note expressively merges with the upbeat pattern upon repetitions of the melody without a pause in lower body movement.

5. Sixteenth notes are contrasted with notes of longer duration. Shorter durations are strong, bound, and direct and rendered staccato (separated, not necessarily short) in movement. Longer durations are light, free, and indirect in movement.
6. Movement accompanying the augmented second (B-natural to A♭) may be declared with anticipation using head, shoulders, and neck. Facial expressions in this regard should not be predictable.
7. Vocal improvisations and creative movement contribute enormously to students' ability to recognize and identify macrobeats and microbeats in performance of a melody. Improvisation and creativity are not limited to one style. With more variability in performance and movement, musicianship becomes broader.

Part 2

Transitioning Learning Sequence Activities to Traditional Activities for Elementary School Instrumental Students Graduating to Upper Grades

Jump Right In: The Instrumental Series is unique. It is predicated on music learning theory and learning sequence activities. The series is designed primarily for students who are beginning to learn to play woodwind, brass, string, and percussion instruments. That is not to say student books and accompanying CDs cannot be used with older students who are beginning instrumental music instruction and have not been exposed to instruction of the traditional type. However, a dilemma arises for many teachers when they contemplate changing teaching procedures with students who have had a year or more of instruction based on traditional methodology to instruction based on music learning theory and learning sequence activities. They believe because of having been exposed to note-naming, counting, music notation, and theoretical information, students will not be capable or even willing to make the change to instruction based on current empirical and observational research. Experience suggests otherwise.

It simply requires a shift from adherence to a theory-laden paradigm to audiation. Thus, the difficulty tends to reside more with the teacher. That is, though the desire may be present, it is because teachers have been indoctrinated with the traditional approach they, themselves, are reluctant to change. The situation is exacerbated when students are expected to make a change without proper guidance. The purpose of Part 2 is to offer teachers encouragement and provide them with information for assisting students who were grounded in music theory in making the transition to instruction integral to music learning theory and learning sequence activities.

Contrasting Audiation, Music Learning Theory, and Learning Sequence Activities with Traditional Instruction

Successful instrumental music teachers are aware of differences among imitation, memorization, and audiation. When students are hearing what they just played and simultaneously hearing what will come next as they are playing, they are audiating. They are making instant generalizations. On the other hand, when students hear only what they are playing as they are playing it, they are imitating through memorization or by reading from note-to-note. Imitation and memorization take place in linear real time. Audiation moves in circular motion, always doubling back on itself to allow performers, as listeners, to anticipate what will be heard in music.

In accord with learning sequence activities, students become proficient on two instruments: their audiation instrument and their actual music instrument. To make satisfactory progress in instrumental music, they first learn their audiation instrument as readiness for learning to play a music instrument. To encourage or allow students to begin studying an actual instrument before their audiation instrument has been developed is unwise. When emphasis is directed toward development of instrumental technique without first teaching audiation skills, students are deprived of necessary foundation for learning to tune their instrument and to play in tune. They will continually be dependent on others to tell them what to do, when to do it, and how to do it.

Traditional beginning instrumental music books emphasize technical skill at the expense of audiation. The books begin by presenting one note at a time rather than patterns of notes. The hope is by learning to play only one note at a time of sustained duration, students will learn the name and fingering of notes, will develop good tone quality as a result of simultaneously learning correct posture and breathing or bowing techniques, and will acquire audiation skill simply through exposure to notation and music theory. Rhythm is virtually ignored, even as students are taught to "hold each note for its full value." When students learn to count one note at a time, isolated time, not contextual musical time, is emphasized. After students are taught individual notes, they are taught to play scales in a variety of keyalities in major tonality long before they are taught to play and read in other tonalities. Moreover, in traditional beginning instrumental music instruction, students are taught to learn fingerings for as many pitches as possible relating to various keyalities in major tonality as they read music notation. Pitches are performed with scales and/or sustained notes rather than collectively in rhythm patterns. Content (individual notes) has dominion over context (tonality, meter, and tempo).

The aforementioned process is not followed when instruction is based on music learning theory. In learning sequence activities, students first learn to play a collection of rhythm patterns in usual duple and usual triple meters in association with only one pitch at a time. Gradually they learn to play several pitches in association with rhythm patterns. That is, they learn melodic patterns, the combining of tonal patterns and rhythm patterns. Students learn tonal patterns in only two or three keyalities in one tonality before they are introduced to a different tonality and different keyalities in that tonality. Reading comes later. Teaching rhythm patterns before tonal patterns and emphasizing tonality over keyality enhances audiation, but not at the expense of technical skill and certainly not at the expense of reading music notation.

The longer students wait to read notation, the more their musicianship develops, because doing so allows them to acquire extensive audiation vocabularies of tonal patterns and rhythm patterns. Regardless of how long reading is postponed, if students learn how to audiate first, they invariably have a desire to learn to read and write notation, and they will quickly be more successful in doing so. If students cannot read unfamiliar patterns with ease, it is probably because they were not adequately taught to read familiar patterns. In other words, they are not able to so-called sight read because they cannot read. It becomes more and more clear there is no such thing as sight reading, because students can either read or cannot read, familiarity or unfamiliarity with patterns notwithstanding.

When students participate in music learning sequence activities in combination with instrumental music activities, they sing songs in major and harmonic minor tonalities and in usual duple and usual triple meters, including those they may have learned or are learning in classroom music. When they are able to audiate major and harmonic minor tonalities and usual duple and usual triple meters, they sing tonic and dominant-seventh patterns in those tonalities and chant macro /microbeat and division patterns in those meters. Then they perform rhythm patterns and tonal patterns, in that order, on instruments.

As a result of learning to audiate tonal patterns using movable-*do* tonal syllables, students audiate relations among pitches instead of emphasizing individual pitches, as when note letter-names are used. Because the same pitch is audiated differently in different keyalities and tonalities, for example, as *do* in one keyality and *so* in another keyality, giving the pitch only one letter name tends to hinder audiation when that pitch is found in different keyalities. On the other hand, the fact the same pitch can have different syllable names in different keyalities seems quite logical to beginning instrumental students who audiate. They know the same pitch can have different syllables associated with it and different pitches may have the same syllable associated with them as a result of singing tonal patterns in various keyalities. Whereas note letter-names are frozen in a fixed system, movable *do*-syllables with a *la-* based minor are flexible and adaptable contextually.

After students develop ability to audiate rhythm patterns in two or more meters using beat-function rhythm syllables, they read music notation with only one measure signature, 2/4, to represent usual duple meter and only one measure signature, 6/8, to represent usual triple meter. The measure signatures 2/4 and 6/8 are used rather than 4/4 and 3/4 because, in addition to beams outlining rhythm patterns, intuitive pairing of macrobeats in audiation can be seen in notation within a measure. After students learn to read rhythm patterns using 2/4 and 6/8, they learn to read the same usual duple meter patterns using a measure signature with a different upper numeral from and the same lower numeral as 2/4, such as 4/4, and then to read the same usual triple meter patterns using a measure signature that has a different upper numeral from and the same lower numeral as 6/8, such as 3/8. Next, measure signatures with different lower numerals and the same upper numerals, such as 2/8 for usual duple meter and 6/4 for usual triple meter, are learned, and finally, measure signatures with different lower and upper numerals, such as 4/8 for usual duple meter and 3/4 for usual triple meter, are introduced. Students are then ready to read rhythm patterns in usual duple and usual triple meters using a variety of measure signatures regardless of combinations of numerals. To read music notation in usual combined meter, the measure signature 2/4 is used initially, and in unusual meters, the measure signatures 5/8 and 7/8 are used initially.

All measure signatures used with usual duple meter are enrhythmic, all measure signatures used with usual triple meter are enrhythmic, and so on for all meters. In learning sequence activities, students do not memorize comparative note values to learn to read using different measure signatures in the same or different meters. Rather, they are guided in discovering how the same rhythm pattern with one measure signature may be translated into another measure signature. When students are not confused by note values and theoretical definitions of numerals in measure signatures, they naturally develop an understanding of rhythm notation. If difficulties are experienced in sustaining consistent tempo as they play, they are not told to count or tap feet. Rather, they stand and move in place or move around the room to macrobeats and microbeats at the correct tempo, using their sense of weight and flow as they respond to musical time through space.

The design and organization of *Jump Right In: The Instrumental Series* facilitates home practice without initial aid of notation. The books include pictures to assist students in developing techniques associated with playing, such as finger-pattern charts that include each syllable in every tonal pattern in the keyalities and tonalities students are learning to perform. A pitch name, not a note letter-name, is associated with the syllable of only the resting tone for each tonality in the keyality students are learning. Pitch names are different from note letter-names. For example, G-*do* is a pitch name that is audiated, whereas G is a note letter-name that is read and seen on the second line of the treble staff. As new tonal patterns and syllables in new keyalities and tonalities are introduced, additional finger patterns are added to charts.

To further facilitate home practice, students are provided with recordings of songs and tonal patterns and rhythm patterns with and without verbal associations they will be learning. They sing songs, perform chants, and sing and chant patterns before they perform patterns and songs on their instruments. Depending on level of learning being taught, students may imitate or audiate some patterns and create or improvise others. In any case, students perform after they hear patterns on the recording, not simultaneously. In time, when they are ready to read, students are encouraged to read music notation. However, they begin to read by associating tonal syllables and rhythm syllables with notation. Note letter-names and time-value names are taught only after students audiate and read music notation fluently using movable-*do* syllables with a *la*-based minor.

Transitional Preparation

Ideally in a well developed music curriculum, what has been taught in lower grades is effectively incorporated into procedures prevalent in upper grades. Realistically and unfortunately, such coordination in music is rarely the case. Thus, to prepare students to make a smooth changeover from education based on music learning theory and learning sequence activities to training of the conventional type, attention to their needs is essential. How well students are prepared for advanced study depends upon a variety of factors including whether you have had them under your guidance for one, two, or three years and the number and length of instructional periods each week. Regardless of scheduling implications, even if they have accomplished comparatively little under your tutelage, music learning theory and learning sequence activities will play a formative role in their interpreting and acclimating unfamiliar types of incremental instruction.

Rapid change seldom endures. To be worthwhile, change must be undertaken gradually. Nevertheless, change is difficult, particularly for older than younger persons. Whereas students are flexible and more willing to experiment with change because they are naturally curious about alternate ways of thinking, it may be expected their new teachers will be somewhat intimidated by not being familiar with knowledge and skills some of their students possess pertaining to music learning theory and learning sequence activities. Many teachers are uninformed about current modes of research and their applications to instructional procedures. After all, teachers who teach the way they were taught or the way they were taught to teach have reason to believe there is no need for change because in their opinion, they are successful in their profession. Their performance groups have probably won prizes and received acceptable ratings at contests, and that supports their decision to sustain a common-practice approach to teaching. Such confidence endures even though they must know the majority of their students, because of insufficient musicianship or boredom, will not participate in instrumental music performance throughout their school years and after graduation. Nonetheless, it is the obligation of professional, mature teachers to acknowledge, accept, and understand pedagogical differences they encounter to assure all students will maintain their self-confidence and sense of self-worth as they progress from one teacher to another.

Different Methods and Teachers

General issues to consider for preparing students to make a smooth transition from learning sequence activities to traditional instruction are outlined below. It is expected you necessarily will contribute other important topics not specifically addressed herein but perhaps are unique to students in your specific school and school system.

1. Explain to students there are different ways to learn the same thing. For example, some teachers use an abacus to teach basic arithmetic, some use manipulatives (small objects that are spread out on a table and then added together or subtracted from one another), others simply use a pencil and paper, and still others believe the best way to solve computation problems is to think them through silently without using visual aids. A lively class discussion comparing how students learned skills in dissimilar ways should help clarify the idea of diversity.

2. Make it clear to students there are different but not necessarily right or wrong ways to learn to play a music instrument. They have been taught one way but there are other ways, and although some ways are superior to others, no one knows for sure which way is best. Teachers choose the method they believe is better. Explain, after careful thought, you decided *Jump Right In: The Instrumental Series* excels in developing musicianship and performance skills.

3. It would be well to tell students they might discover their new teacher has not used and/or is unfamiliar with *Jump Right In: The Instrumental Series*. That is not necessarily bad because unless contradictory, the more ways students are taught something, the better they will understand it. They can be sure the way you have taught them is not fundamentally in musical conflict with the way the new teacher thinks. Further, the way they have been taught probably includes skills the new teacher does not intend to teach. What they already know will not only help them understand new concepts they will be learning, what they will be learning will also help them better understand what they have already learned from you.

4. Advise students to respect the new teacher and not reject new ideas that he or she presents. Further, it would not be prudent for them to interrupt the new teacher during class to offer an

explanation about how they were previously taught. Rather, they should use their time valuably by quietly applying what they are being taught to what they have already learned. Explain you are going to assist them in a practical manner to understand how that is accomplished.

5. Approximately two weeks before the end of the school year, before students are to begin studying with a new teacher, spend a portion of each class period explaining conventional music terminology, even if one or more students have familiarity with some of its elements. Prepare packets of two or three pages for individual students, it may be titled Music Theory, and include the following content. Music symbols, key signatures, note letter-names, dynamic and tempo markings, note-value names and corresponding rests, measure signatures, and a potpourri of common symbols and terms associated with music notation. Spend time offering a swift explanation of each entry in the packet. Tell students it is not necessary to memorize what is in the packet. They will naturally become familiar with meanings and definitions as they perform on their instruments and read music notation. However, they may want to make occasional reference to the material during summer vacation and coming school years. A suggested chart of what may be included in the packet is presented below. Reproduce the chart if desired.

Music Symbols

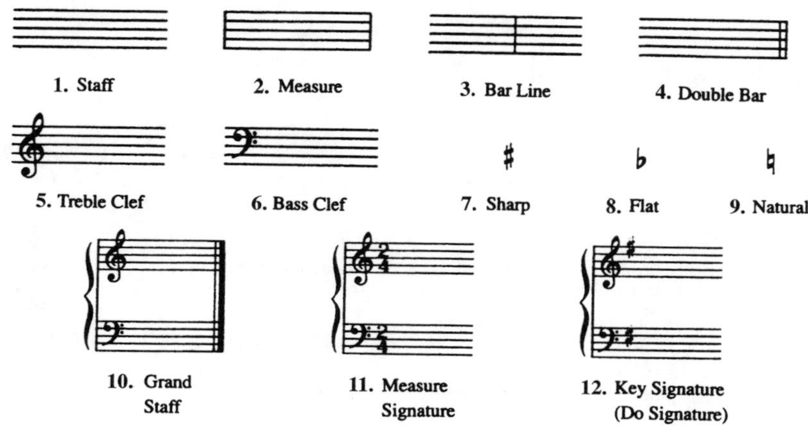

Key Signatures

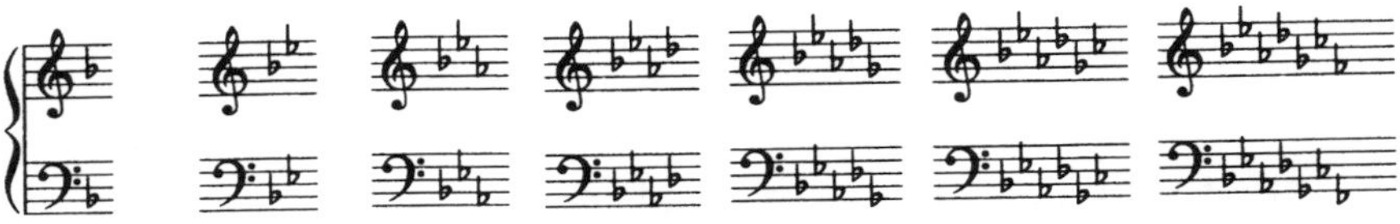

F Major D Minor G Dorian C Mixolydian (F is Do)	B♭ Major G Minor C Dorian F Mixolydian (B♭ is Do)	E♭ Major C Minor F Dorian B♭ Mixolydian (E♭ is Do)	A♭ Major F Minor B♭ Dorian E♭ Mixolydian (A♭ is Do)	D♭ Major B♭ Minor E♭ Dorian A♭ Mixolydian (D♭ is Do)	G♭ Major E♭ Minor A♭ Dorian D♭ Mixolydian (G♭ is Do)	C♭ Major A♭ Minor D♭ Dorian G♭ Mixolydian (C♭ is Do)
G Major E Minor A Dorian D Mixolydian (G is Do)	D Major B Minor E Dorian A Mixolydian (D is Do)	A Major F♯ Minor B Dorian E Mixolydian (A is Do)	E Major C♯ Minor F♯ Dorian B Mixolydian (E is Do)	B Major G♯ Minor C♯ Dorian F♯ Mixolydian (B is Do)	F♯ Major D♯ Minor G♯ Dorian C♯ Mixolydian (F♯ is Do)	C♯ Major A♯ Minor D♯ Dorian G♯ Mixolydian (C♯ is Do)

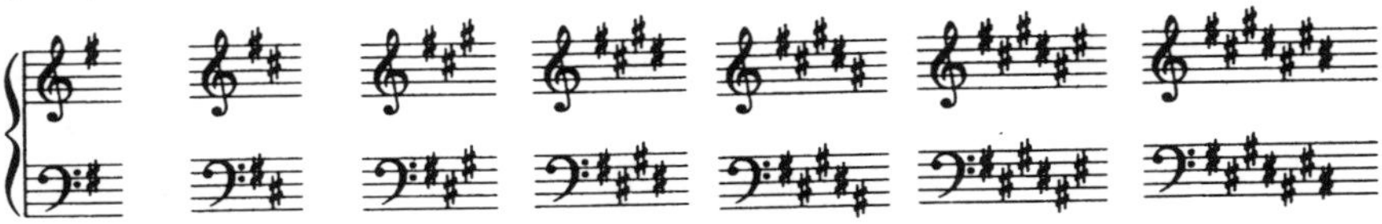

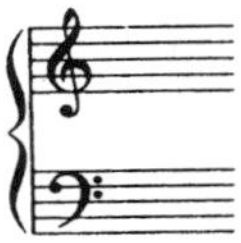

C Major
A Minor
D Dorian
G Mixolydian
(C is Do)

Measure Signatures

$\frac{2}{4}$	$\frac{4}{4}$	¢	$\frac{6}{8}$	$\frac{3}{8}$	$\frac{3}{4}$
1. Two-four	2. Four-four	3. alla breve (cut time)	4. Six-eight	5. Three-eight	6. Three-four

Note Names/Rest Names

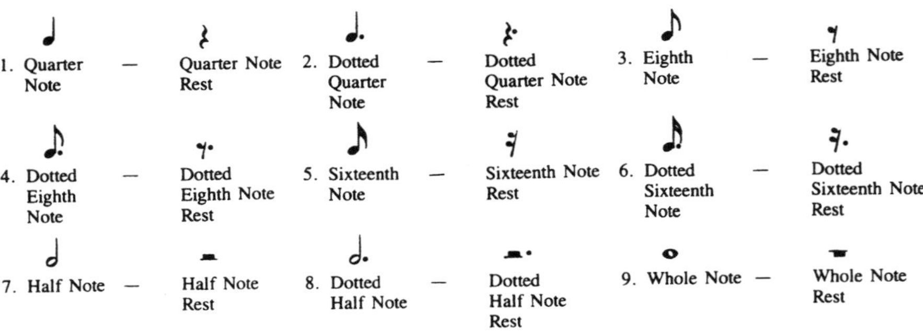

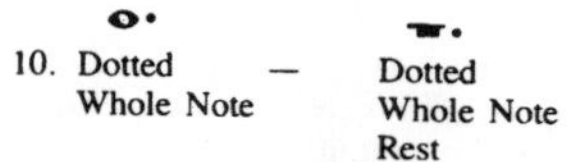

Note Letter Names

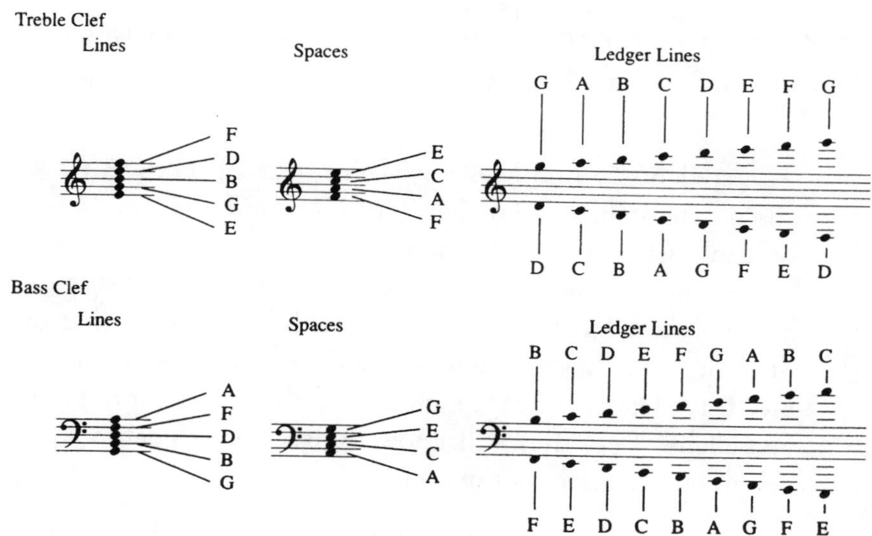

Dynamic/Tempo Markings

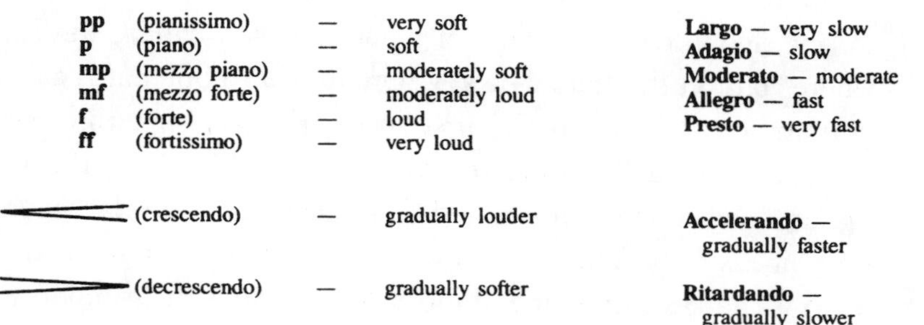

pp	(pianissimo)	—	very soft
p	(piano)	—	soft
mp	(mezzo piano)	—	moderately soft
mf	(mezzo forte)	—	moderately loud
f	(forte)	—	loud
ff	(fortissimo)	—	very loud
	(crescendo)	—	gradually louder
	(decrescendo)	—	gradually softer

Largo — very slow
Adagio — slow
Moderato — moderate
Allegro — fast
Presto — very fast

Accelerando — gradually faster

Ritardando — gradually slower

Other Music Terms

1. **D.C. (Da Capo)** — go back to the beginning.
2. **D.S. (Dal Segno)** — go back to the sign (𝄋).
3. **Fine** — end.
4. **Coda** — closing section of piece.
5. **D.C. al fine** — go back to the beginning and play to the Fine.
6. **D.S. al fine** — go back to the sign (𝄋) and play to the Fine.
7. **D.C. al Coda** — go back to the beginning and play to the Coda Sign (𝄋), and then skip to the Coda.
8. **D.S. al Coda** — go back to the sign (𝄋) and play to the Coda Sign (𝄌), and then skip to the Coda.

6. Ask students to find *Music Symbols* in their packet. After you discuss the staff, measure, bar lines, clefs, and accidentals, some students will ask why learning all these names are necessary. Agree they already know how to interpret their meanings in performance, but to communicate with the new teacher and students who have attended other elementary schools, they need to learn their language, which is common among musicians. True, they will know things other students do not know, but that does not matter.

7. Look at *Key Signatures*. Explain *do*-signatures will be called key signatures. Nonetheless, as they learned when they were told where to place their fingers on instruments for *B♭-do*, *C-do*, and so on, signatures, regardless of what they are called, indicate where *do* is on the staff. The key signature with one flat is called F. It indicates *do* is on the first space; the key signature with two flats, called B♭, indicates *do* is on the third line; the key signature with one sharp, called G, indicates *do* is on the second line; and so on. The only new thing students might need to learn is the keyality name of more *do* signatures. It is important to emphasize despite how signatures are defined, they are read the same familiar way. Remind students a key signature may be used to indicate major tonality, minor tonality, Dorian tonality, and so on. Also, prepare students to expect the possibility some teachers will combine keyality and tonality when they talk about key signatures. That is, they might say B♭ major.

   Direct students' attention to the measure signature under *Music Symbols*. Their new teacher will probably call it a time signature or meter signature, but that is of no concern because they already know what the numbers indicate. Remind students when they see 2/4 44, C, or ¢ it means music will be audiated in duple meter. When they see 6/8 or 3/4 it means music will be audiated in triple meter.

8. Look at *Measure Signatures*. Their new teacher will most likely call 2/4, two-four; 4/4 and C, four-four; ¢, alla breve or cut time; 6/8, six-eight; 3/8, three-eight; and 3/4, three-four. It is not necessary to go into great detail or offer explanations about fractions and note values. They serve no immediate practical purpose. Your responsibility is to familiarize students with names they will need to know in the near future to communicate with their new teacher. If students are directed to memorize, they will quickly forget what they do not forthwith use. What they might not know, they will learn as they participate in ensemble activities. In fact, students who were taught traditionally will become fascinated with your students and want to know what they know. The exchange of information among students will fill many gaps in understanding different music languages.

9. Look at *Note Names/Rest Names*. Their new teacher will talk about beats in a measure. As explained, a measure includes notes between two bar lines. For example, the teacher might say there are two beats in a 2/4 measure. Macrobeats in 2/4 will be called quarter notes, and microbeats in 2/4 will be called eighth notes. Also, macrobeat and microbeat rests in 2/4 will be called quarter-note and eighth-note rests. In 6/8, macrobeats will be called dotted-quarter notes and microbeats will be called eighth-notes. Follow through offering an overview of other note names and rests. Avoid pedantic explanations.

10. Look at Note *Letter Names*. Now it can be explained that each line and space on the staff has a letter name. Explain again to students note letter-names match pitch names learned to place fingers properly for each *do*. For example, *B♭-do* and *E♭-do*. Again, it is not necessary for students to memorize these names. The will quickly be assimilated by listening to remarks of their

teacher during performance rehearsals. Nonetheless, it would be prudent to assist students in associating note letter-names with solfege. For example, if the key signature is ***B♭***, F is *so*, D is *mi*, ***B♭*** is *do*, and so on. That should be sufficient to allow students to participate in rehearsals and garner confidence necessary for understanding directions and requests.

11. Look at *Dynamic/Tempo Markings*, *Other Music Symbols*, and *Other Music Terms*. A cursory survey of meanings of markings, symbols, and terms is all that is undertaken. It is assured new teachers will necessarily and constantly be reminding students how to attend to them. Soon meanings will become common through use. Conductor/teachers of amateur performance ensembles agree periodic explanations and reminders are a natural consequence of educational accountability.

12. Students may put the packet away for safe keeping and future use. Now select a piece of familiar or unfamiliar music notation, in either major or harmonic minor tonality, in the treble clef. All students should have a copy. First, arbitrarily identify some tonal patterns and together with students, read and sing them using movable-*do* syllables. Then, start at the beginning of the notation and recite **(speak, not sing)** individual note letter-names on the staff. Continue the game-like activity until students understand the system of associating letter-names with lines and spaces. Follow the same procedure using notation in bass clef.

13. Using the same or different music notation in duple meter, arbitrarily identify some rhythm patterns and together with students, read and chant them using beat-function rhythm syllables. Body movement should not be discouraged. Then, start at the beginning of the music notation and recite **(speak, not chant)** individual time-value names on the staff. Continue the game-like activity until students understand the system of associating time-value names with notes. Follow the same procedure using notation in triple meter.

14. Finally, an amicable discussion with students is in order. Explain some of their new friends will know valuable things they don't know but many will not understand or know how to audiate. When explaining differences between audiation and notation to their peers, they should be tolerant, gracious, and open-minded on all occasions. It is important students not abandon what they have learned. They should maintain skills, especially audiation, because they represent a significant part of musicianship. In fact, students may find it necessary to audiate tonal syllables and rhythm syllables to solve notational problems for themselves.

15. It is possible with a change of instruction students will lose motivation to learn and to continue to participate in instrumental music. Their possible boredom may be abated by encouraging them to continue improvising individually and with friends. They may continue to use CDs provided with *Jump Right In: The Instrumental Series* for that purpose. Perhaps what might be found to be most compelling for sustaining their interest and motivation in instrumental music is when they form and become members of small instrumental ensembles (duets, trios, quartets, quintets, and so on.) Undoubtedly, their new teacher will be delighted to assist them in that endeavor, because it will be to the advantage of all.

Part 3

Introducing Middle and High School Instrumental Students to Learning Sequence Activities

The focus of Part 2 is to guide elementary school music teachers in assisting students who were taught beginning instrumental music based on principles of music learning theory and learning sequence activities to make the transition to traditional instruction as they moved into middle school and beyond. After elementary school instrumental music teachers prepared students for change and once students graduated to upper grades, responsibility for students making a smooth and responsible transition resided with middle school instrumental music teachers. Elementary instrumental music teachers who are aware of the value of music learning theory and learning sequence activities are no longer in control and thus, cannot oversee the transition. Faith and hope rather than action become the only options. Now, in Part 3, the situation is reversed. Middle and high school instrumental music teachers who are aware of the value of music learning theory and learning sequence activities are in control. That is an important distinction between the two conditions, because now teachers responsible for currently guiding students through positive change play a direct active role in the endeavor. Reliance and trust alone are no longer crucial issues.

Transitional Preparation

Results of a music aptitude test will serve you in garnering valuable knowledge about students you will be teaching. Either the *Musical Aptitude Profile* or the *Advanced Measures of Music Audiation* is recommended for administration. Information pertaining to these and other tests may be found in the following titles, also by Edwin E. Gordon: *Introduction to Research and the Psychology of Music* and *Music Aptitude and Related Tests* (G-5719), a brochure published by GIA and offered free of charge. Both publications are listed in the Bibliography. Test results will guide you in teaching to individual musical differences among students. When students' individual musical needs are taken into account, those with limited potential will not become frustrated and others with exceptional potential will not become bored. Preliminary time spent reading test manuals and ancillary books about the interpretation and use of music aptitude test results will be rewarding.

Before going into detail regarding pedagogical procedures, a few caveats are in order. To be forewarned is to be forearmed. Regardless of your interest and dedication to music learning theory and learning sequence activities and your desire to provide students with what you believe to be high standards of music education, problems will arise with a minority of students. Those students, who often possess low potential for learning music, will not be particularly interested in developing their musicianship. They are more interested in entertainment and social benefits than a substantial education in music. Fear and laziness will prompt them to protest suggested change from a familiar, perhaps rote, routine to what they consider to be an intrusion on their complacency. Thus, although you spend time and effort in answering their questions and hoping to motivate them, the result with some will prove to be of no avail. Their complaints will persist and eventually lead to a discontinuation of their participation in the instrumental ensemble. If school administrators evaluate your teaching effectiveness according to enrollment statistics, you may find yourself in a difficult position if you are not prepared for such an eventuality. Take time beforehand to explain to school officials your plan for educating students, how possible initial problems will eventually result in benefits for the school as well as students. In fact, enrollment probably will ultimately increase, because students will share their excitement with friends when they discover they need not consult their instrument to hear what music notation sounds like. They will have gone beyond mere note-naming and will have learned how to audiate. They will become obsessed with their own improvisations, compositions, and arrangements.

Above all, do not become discouraged. Your obvious dedication and persistence will not go unnoticed by students. Soon they will acquire an uncommon joy of learning about and participating in music performance. The romance of music will reach lofty levels by replacing drill and memorization with improvisation and creativity.

General issues to consider for sensitively introducing students who have been taught music conventionally to music learning theory and learning sequence activities are outlined below. It is expected you will necessarily contribute other important topics not specifically addressed herein but are perhaps unique to your students and the established curriculum.

Explain to students you are interested in spending time with them to investigate benefits of a new approach to learning music. You believe it will broaden them musically by increasing their musical skills and knowledge. However, to achieve the goal, you will need their cooperation and assistance. They can help by listening carefully, being open-minded and patient with themselves, and offering you astute positive criticism. Assure them you will arrange sessions for interaction of your and their ideas, but they must remember progress in their musicianship may not be immediate.

By learning to audiate, they will be able to look at music notation and hear it in their minds before playing it on an instrument. In that way, by audiating what they are going to play before they play it, music notation can be performed with superior intonation and rhythm in the band or orchestra. Further, audiation is the basis of improvisation and composition. If you and they are successful in this new endeavor, in addition to participating in large school ensembles, they can become contributing members of small groups and play various types of popular music without aid of music notation and with satisfaction. In time they may also be capable of composing and arranging their own music they and others will enjoy performing.

It may not be reasonable to use *Jump Right In: The Instrumental Series* books designed specifically for beginners with older advanced students. Those books are intended primarily for students who are first learning to play a music instrument in elementary school. Your imagination and ingenuity along with the following ideas and suggestions should be sufficient. However, as will be explained, use of supplementary CDs that enhance *Jump Right In: The Instrumental Series* will be of enormous value in guiding students in audiation activities. Also, *Jump Right In: The Instrumental Series* books for students to create their own compositions may be used. How you might author similar material for your students will be explained.

An entire period should not be directed toward learning sequence activities. In the beginning, perhaps ten minutes or so, preferably at the onset or end of each period, might be appropriate. That is, do not attempt an abrupt total alteration of methodology. The change from common-practice schooling to current research-based instruction should be gradual over a period of learning sequence activity sessions. Both types of teaching are undertaken simultaneously. Initially, traditional activities will assume the majority of class time. Once students realize the practicality and value of music learning theory and learning sequence activities, the majority of class time will naturally be magnetized to principles embedded in those concepts. A new world of possibilities for making music will inspire students. They will be captured by endless potentialities. Soon, amid other bonuses, students will intuit their newly acquired abilities to audiate and improvise has improved their ability to read music notation artistically and to tune their instruments in a professional manner.

Pedagogy

Tonal Development

1. Empirical research and experience indicate, and fine musicians agree, singing improves one's ability to play a music instrument in tune. My research goes further. It seems clear students rarely learn to play a music instrument with unblemished intonation any better than they sing or have sung with trustworthy intonation. After all, how do students know they are playing out of tune unless they are able to compare what they are playing with what they have sung and as a result are able to audiate. Succinctly, singing begets substantial audiation. Think of string students who need tape attached to fingerboards of their instruments. Because they cannot audiate, they must attempt to "touch" or "feel" intonation. It may barely solve an immediate problem but unfortunately, students usually are incapable of generalizing the illusive panacea.

2. It is, of course, much easier to convince elementary than middle and high school students to sing. There are various reasons why older students have a negative attitude toward singing. If males whose voices are changing or have changed have not sung in tune using their unchanged voice, it is difficult if not impossible now for them to learn to sing in tune. Because of sensitivity, they will not make an attempt for fear of embarrassment, and that is understandable. Rather than forcing them to sing, it might be better for them to listen to and assimilate the quality of singing of capable female and male classmates. However, it is recommended they be given special attention when the class is introduced to moving and chanting rhythm. Albeit, there are able students, including males and females, who insist they joined a band or orchestra to perform on an instrument but not to sing. It takes time and charismatic persuasion to convince them of the value of continuing to sing but nonetheless, the challenge must somehow be successfully pursued.

   During learning sequence activities, students engage in unison class singing. Familiar short songs in major and harmonic minor tonalities and usual duple and triple meters are best. A suitable tessitura is from D above middle C to A or B♭, a fifth or minor sixth above, and the prevailing range is from D above middle C to E, a tenth above. It is of extreme importance to firmly establish context, in terms of tonality, keyality, beginning pitch, meter, and tempo, of each song before students begin to sing.

3. Once students become comfortable with unison ensemble singing, they begin to sing tonal patterns as an ensemble. Solo singing may take place later if desired. Be certain to firmly establish tonality and keyality in which tonal patterns are to be sung before students begin to sing. That might be accomplished by you and/or the class singing a short song.

   It is not necessary to coordinate tonal patterns students will be singing with tonal patterns found in music they are performing or will be performing instrumentally. Any arrangements of tonic and dominant-seventh patterns, and later subdominant patterns, in major and harmonic tonalities are appropriate. Take a deep breath as a model before you sing a two, usually a three, or rarely a four note tonal pattern for the class. After a short pause allowing students to audiate the pattern but not long enough to memorize it, students take a deep breath and repeat the pattern. Keep the process going by interchanging tonic and dominant-seventh tonal patterns, occasionally pausing to emphasize through performance the tonic pitch. Make all pitches in a tonal pattern the same length to insure patterns do not suggest or convey a specific rhythm or meter.

4. It is advisable to initiate singing of tonal patterns by using one or more neutral syllables, such as *bum*. As soon as workable, sing familiar tonal patterns using movable-*do* syllables. For a tonic pattern in major tonality, sing any combination of *do mi so*; for a dominant-seventh pattern in major tonality, any combination of *so ti re fa*; and for a subdominant pattern in major tonality, any combination of *fa la do*. For a tonic pattern in harmonic minor tonality, sing any combination of *la do mi*; for a dominant-

seventh pattern in harmonic minor tonality, any combination of *mi si ti re*; and for a subdominant pattern in harmonic minor tonality, any combination of *re fa la.* Inversions are recommended for smooth voice leadings. (An ascending chromatic scale using movable-*do* syllables is *do di re ri mi fa fi so si la li ti do*; descending, *do ti te la le so se fa mi me re ra do.*)

5. Though it is not necessary to explain the following to students, it may be helpful for you to understand why movable *do*-syllables with a *la* based minor are indispensable for learning how to audiate. First, when *do* is audiated as tonic, students know without resorting to music theory or notation music is in major tonality; when *la* is audiated as tonic, music is in harmonic minor or Aeolian tonality; when *re* is audiated as tonic, music is in Dorian tonality; when *mi* is audiated as tonic, music is in Phrygian tonality; when *fa* is audiated as tonic, music is in Lydian tonality; when *so* is audiated as tonic, music is in Mixolydian tonality; and when *ti* is audiated as tonic, music is in Locrian tonality. Second, as explained, note letter-names are a fixed system, whereas syllables are a movable system. Regardless in the fixed system whether, for example, B♭ is audiated as *do* or *fa* in a keyality, it is still called B♭. That contradicts audiation and yields to music theory and notation. With syllables, that is not the case. The syllable name of the same pitch changes according to its function in a keyality. Thus, students' capability of learning how to audiate is enhanced with rapidity.

6. Introduce names of tonalities (major and harmonic minor) and pattern functions (tonic, dominant, and subdominant) casually in a practical manner during learning sequence activities. It is not necessary to resort to music notation and/or expound on music theory. As in most learning, names are commonly applied without explaining the source of the names. Simply associate labels with sound. When students begin to improvise, they discover practical knowledge of names of tonalities and pattern functions to be of enormous assistance. Functional use becomes a reality when not stifled by theoretical information.

BRASS, WOODWIND, AND MALLET INSTRUMENTS

7. In major tonality and D keyality, sing a succession of tonal patterns, taking a deep breath before performing them and making short pauses between them, and ask students to repeat them by singing one at a time. After students have sung and become familiar with a dozen or so tonal patterns in major tonality, they repeat the tonal patterns in unison in major tonality and B♭ concert keyality one at a time on their instruments. Because tonal patterns are being played instrumentally in another keyality, firmly establish the new keyality in major tonality before you sing or play tonal patterns students are to repeat. Students will have no problem singing in one keyality and performing instrumentally in another.

   Depending on instruments being used in the ensemble, quickly remind students of fingerings for B♭-*do*, C-*do*, E♭-*do*, and/or F-*do* on their various instruments. Next, explain how *re* is fingered. Do not call it C or D etc. Other than for *do*, give instructions using only syllable names. Percussion students are shown placement of C-*do* and relevant syllables on keyboard or mallet instruments. Students instrumentally imitate a variety of tonal patterns including only *do* and *re* in familiar rhythm patterns. Soon fingerings for *ti*, *mi*, and *fa* are similarly introduced in additional familiar rhythm patterns. As you wish, guide students in performing both diatonic and arpeggio tonal patterns. If you do not sing patterns using tonal syllables for students to imitate instrumentally, avoid allowing them to watch how your fingers move on an instrument.

8. After singing a series of tonal patterns in major tonality and D keyality, follow the same procedure in major tonality and E♭ concert keyality. If students find the idea confusing that *do* can be associated with different pitches, sing the same song with them in two keyalities. That should reinforce the nature of transposition, that E♭, for example, can be *fa* in one keyality and *do* in another. The range of an octave is now available and thus, songs with more extensive ranges may be performed

instrumentally through audiation. Remind students in major tonality, *ti* in B♭ concert keyality is fingered differently from *fa* in E♭ concert keyality.

9. Progress now to guiding students in audiating familiar songs and then perform them without aid of notation in one or more keyalities. They will quickly learn to transpose with ease, shunning customary fear of music theory. The only essentials you give them are the fingering for *do* and the syllable name for the beginning pitch of the song.

10. In harmonic minor tonality and D keyality, sing a succession of tonal patterns, taking a deep breath before performing them and making short pauses between them, and ask students to repeat them one at a time. Then establish harmonic minor tonality and G keyality (the relative minor of B♭ concert keyality), and ask students to repeat tonal patterns you sing or play on their instruments. Depending on instruments being used in the ensemble, show them fingerings for G *la*, A *la*, C *la*, and/or D *la* on the various instruments. Next, explain how *si* is fingered. Do not call it F♯. Other than for *la*, give instructions using only syllable names. Students instrumentally imitate a variety of tonal patterns including only *la* and *ti* in familiar rhythm patterns. Soon fingerings for *si*, *do*, and *re* are similarly introduced. As you wish, guide students in performing both diatonic and arpeggio tonal patterns in additional familiar rhythm patterns. Progress now to guiding students in audiating familiar songs and performing them instrumentally without aid of notation in one or more keyalities. Their ability to transpose with ease will be reinforced. The only essentials you give them are the fingering for *la* and the syllable name for the first pitch of the song.

11. After singing a series of tonal patterns in harmonic minor tonality and D keyality, follow the same procedure with instrumental performance in harmonic tonality and C concert keyality (the relative minor of E♭ major concert keyality). As

with *do*, students will quickly understand that *la* can be associated with any pitch if you sing the same song with them in two keyalities. That should reinforce their understanding of transposition. C can be *re* in one keyality and *la* in another. With this accomplished, the range of an octave is available and thus, songs with more extensive ranges may be performed through audiation. In harmonic minor tonality, *si* in G concert keyality is fingered differently from *fa* in C concert keyality.

STRING INSTRUMENTS

12. Review suggestions 1 through 6.

13. First establishing major tonality and D keyality, either play or sing a succession of tonal patterns, taking a deep breath before performing and making short pauses between them. Ask students to repeat them by singing one at a time. After students have sung and become familiar with a dozen or so tonal patterns in major tonality, they play the tonal patterns in unison one at a time on their instruments. Quickly remind them of the fingering for D *do* on their various instruments. Because violin, viola, cello, and double bass are non-transposing instruments (except for double bass which sounds one octave lower than notation), all students perform in unison in the same keyality. Next, explain how *re* is fingered. Do not call it E. Other than for *do*, give instructions using only syllable names. Students instrumentally imitate a variety of tonal patterns including *do* and *re* in familiar rhythm patterns. Soon fingerings for *ti*, *mi*, and *fa* are similarly introduced. As you wish, guide students in performing both diatonic and arpeggio tonal patterns. If you do not sing patterns using tonal syllables for students to imitate instrumentally, avoid allowing them to watch how your fingers move on an instrument.

14. After singing a series of tonal patterns in major tonality and D keyality, follow the same procedure in major tonality and G keyality. If students find the idea confusing that *do* can be associated with various pitches, sing the same song with them in

two keyalities. That should reinforce the nature of transposition, that G, for example, can be *fa* in one keyality and *do* in another. With this accomplished, the range of an octave is available and thus, songs with more extensive ranges may be performed instrumentally through audiation. Remind students in major tonality, *ti* in D keyality is fingered differently from *fa* in G keyality.

15. Progress now to guiding students in audiating familiar songs and then performing them without aid of notation in one or more keyalities. They will quickly learn to transpose with ease, shunning customary fear of music theory. The only essentials you give them are the location of *do* and the syllable name for the beginning pitch of the song.

16. After singing a series of tonal patterns in harmonic minor tonality and D keyality, follow the same procedure with instrumental performance in harmonic minor tonality and G keyality (the parallel minor of G major keyality). Show students the location of G *la* on their various instruments. Next, explain how *si* is fingered. Do not call it F#. Other than for *la*, give instructions using only syllable names. Students instrumentally imitate a variety of tonal patterns including *la* and *ti* in familiar rhythm patterns. Soon fingerings for *si*, *do*, and *re* are similarly introduced. As you wish, guide students in performing both diatonic and arpeggio tonal patterns in familiar rhythm patterns.

17. Progress now to guiding students in audiating familiar songs and then performing them instrumentally without aid of notation in one or more keyalities. That should reinforce their understanding of transposition. The only essentials you give them are the fingering for *la* and the syllable name for the first pitch of the song. Depending on interest and capability of the class and/or individual students, additional keyalities in harmonic minor tonality may be introduced.

Rhythm Development

1. As discussed in Part 1, *Movement and Interactive Breathing as Readiness for Learning Rhythm*, most students have been taught to count numbers as a means of learning rhythm. Although students correctly name numbers, they do not always recite them at appropriate times. Teachers often suggest foot tapping, but that intensifies the problem. Foot muscles become tense and tempos unsteady. The situation becomes obvious as tempos rush and slow, individual notes are given improper duration, and rhythm is distorted. Performance after a rest is begun too late or too early.

   Unfortunately, students are taught time before they are guided in experiencing space. It is feeling of space through body movement that indicates to students when consecutive beats are to occur. Counting is unnecessary, if not counterproductive. Once students are comfortable moving in space with supportive breath, either by standing in place or moving around the room and activating upper and/or lower parts of their body, they begin to impose musical time on space. That is accomplished by internalizing a feeling of space as beats are properly placed in the flow of musical time. Students learn to "audiate" space as they perform tempo, meter, and rhythm in accordance with beat placement.

2. Research and experience indicate physical movement improves students' ability to play a music instrument with consistency of tempo, stability of meter, and accurate rhythm. Further, it seems clear students will not learn to play a music instrument with good rhythm any better than they physically move with good rhythm. A most efficient, and possibly the sole, way of developing sufficient rhythm audiation is to move. The reason so many musically inexperienced students perform with unreliable rhythm is because they do not audiate rhythmically.

3. It is, of course, much easier to convince elementary than middle and high school students to move. Whereas young children are cooperative and enthusiastic about participating in movement

activities, for whatever the reasons older students are inhibited when asked to move their bodies though they appear not to have these inhibitions when dancing to popular music. Thus, it usually is necessary to divert their attention away from the primary goal of having them move in a relaxed and free-flowing continuous manner. A perusal of the pedagogy offered for each of the more than twenty melodies in Part 1 should provide various ideas for achieving the desired intent. However, because the exact same techniques are inappropriate for older and younger students, activities are adapted to the sophistication accompanying increased chronological age. Rather than focusing student's attention on movement, create games in which students engage in free-flowing continuous movement as they play the game. For example, groups of four or five students in a circle throw a small ball to one another, always moving in a free-flowing continuous manner regardless of whether they are idle, throwing, or catching the ball. If an individual stops moving, the game ceases momentarily and their team loses a point. Ongoing scores are recorded for all to see. The game begins again and a student or you continue to keep score. Another game is, while continuously moving, students as a group audiate and initiate a jump on the fourth macrobeat of a series of four underlying macrobeats and land on the first macrobeat of the next series of four underlying macrobeats. The object of the game is to touch someone but not be touched yourself during the next series of underlying macrobeats. The one who is touched loses a point and freezes as the game continues without a pause. The rivalry of teams of girls against boys is quite effective. It will be discovered students' concern is on winning the game. They tend not to realize they are moving in the desired manner. One benefit of such a game is students are moving together, no one is moving alone for others to observe.

4. During time used for learning sequence activities, students continue to engage in unison class singing of familiar short songs in major and harmonic minor tonalities and usual duple and

triple meters. Procedures, tessituras, and ranges for singing have been described under Tonal Development. More important, however, is students perform chants of four to eight measures long. Once they become comfortable with unison ensemble chanting, students begin to chant rhythm patterns as an ensemble. Be certain to firmly establish meter and tempo at which the rhythm patterns are to be chanted before students begin to chant patterns. That might be accomplished by performing a chant.

It is not necessary to coordinate rhythm patterns students will be chanting with rhythm patterns found in music they are performing or will perform instrumentally. Any macro/microbeat, division, elongation, division/elongation, rest, upbeat, and tie patterns are appropriate. Take a deep breath as a model before you begin to chant. After a short pause that allows students to audiate the pattern but not long enough for them to memorize it, students take a deep breath and they repeat the pattern. Chant all durations in a rhythm pattern on approximately the same pitch to insure patterns do not suggest or convey diatonic intervals or a specific keyality or tonality. Of course, durations in patterns are chanted with artistic expression.

5. You may find it necessary to initiate chanting of rhythm patterns by using one or more neutral syllables, such as *bah*. Although you and students take a deep breath before a series of rhythm patterns is performed, there is no pause, only a breath, between your chanting of each pattern and students' repetition of the pattern. In that way, tempo remains steady.

   As soon as workable, chant familiar rhythm patterns using beat-function rhythm syllables. The rationale of why rhythm syllables based on beat functions rather than on note values are used is presented in Part 1 in association with Melody 23. Also, beat-function rhythm syllables are described and notated under Pedagogy for Melody 23. It is best to begin chanting with macro/microbeat and division patterns in usual duple and triple meters. Once students are comfortable with these, elongations, rest, and upbeat patterns may be introduced. Tie patterns are undertaken last. Finally, all functions of patterns in usual combined meter may be chanted. Examples of rhythm patterns in usual duple, triple, and combined meters are notated below. For a complete presentation of rhythm patterns, see my book, *Rhythm: Contrasting the Implications of Audiation and Notation* listed in the Bibliography.

6. Introduce names of meters (usual duple, triple, and combined) and pattern functions (macro/microbeat, division, elongation, divisions/elongations rest, upbeat, and tie) casually in a practical manner during learning sequence activities. It is not necessary to resort to music notation and/or expound on music theory. As in most learning, names are commonly applied without explaining the source of the names. Simply associate labels with sound. When students begin to improvise, they will discover knowledge of names of meters and pattern functions to be of enormous assistance.

USUAL DUPLE

USUAL TRIPLE

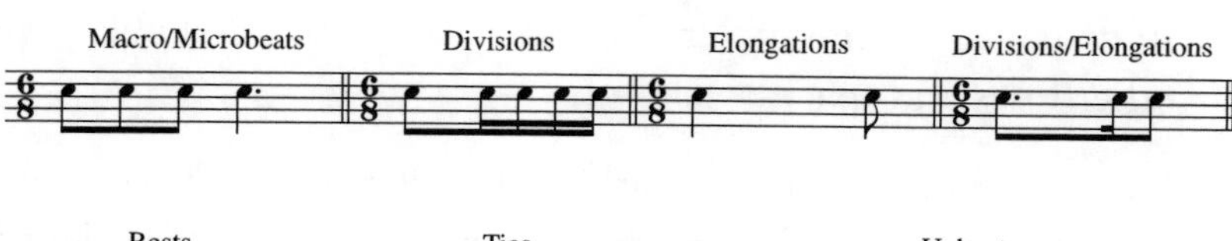

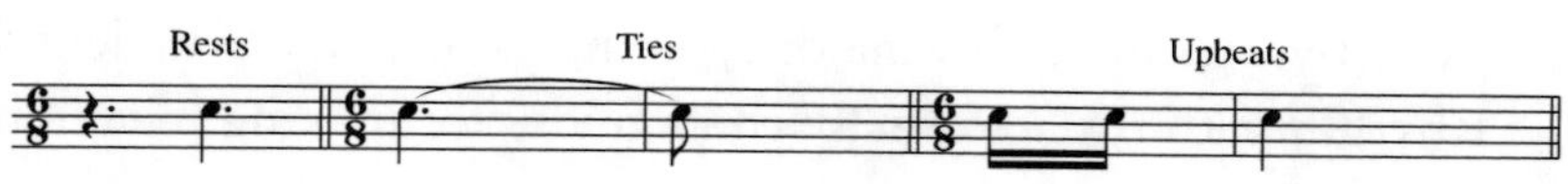

USUAL COMBINED

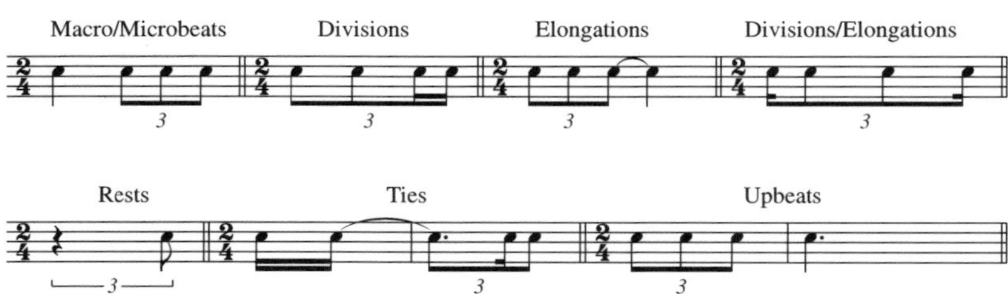

Vocal and Instrumental Notational Audiation

For information to supplement and expand the following outlined procedures for vocally and instrumentally reading and writing music notation, read my book, *The Aural/Visual Experience of Music Literacy*. It is listed in the Bibliography.

Tonal Patterns

1. Select and perform a familiar or unfamiliar short melody of the difficulty level students are able to follow or read using note letter-names. The primary purpose is to establish tonality and keyality for students before they begin to read notation vocally and instrumentally using movable-*do* syllables.

2. Remind students of where *do* is placed on the staff with either the treble or bass clef. Sing *do* with students and explain if *do* is on a line, *mi* and *so* will be on the next two lines above and *ti* on the space below. Similarly, if *do* is on a space, *mi* and *so* will be on the next two spaces above and *ti* is on the line below. Assist students, as necessary, in logically associating syllables with other lines and spaces.

3. You and students together arbitrarily identify tonal patterns of from two to four, the majority being three, notes in length. Rhythm patterns are usually good guides for making selections, but choices need not coincide with what you will later decide upon as being rhythm patterns.

4. You and students together read by singing each tonal pattern one at a time using movable-*do* syllables. Separate tonal patterns and take a deep breath before each is performed. Be certain all pitches are of equal duration so as to not convey rhythm or meter.

5. Soon after students understand the logic of placement of syllables on the staff, guide them in identifying by themselves remaining tonal patterns. Individual students take turns in selecting tonal patterns for the class to read in ensemble.

6. Now the class reads all tonal patterns in the melody one at a time from beginning to end using movable-*do* syllables. Pauses and deep breaths are still observed.

7. After you have notated parts to accommodate transpositions and ranges of instruments in the band or orchestra, conduct students as they read in unison and perform instrumentally all tonal patterns in the melody one at a time from beginning to end, making pauses and taking deep breaths between the patterns. All pitches in a tonal pattern are of equal duration so as not to indicate meter or rhythm. Emphasize, for further development of their musicianship, importance of audiating and associating tonal syllables with fingerings when reading and not habitually decoding note letter-names.

Rhythm Patterns

1. Select and perform a familiar or unfamiliar short melody (it may be the same one already used to read tonal patterns) of the difficulty level students are able to follow or read using note-value names. Notation with an abundance of beams rather than flags is preferable. The primary purpose is to establish meter and tempo for students before they begin to read notation vocally and instrumentally using beat-function rhythm syllables.

2. Remind students of, and demonstrate if necessary through movement, the nature of macrobeats, microbeats, and rhythm patterns. Assist students in logically associating rhythm syllables

with macrobeats, microbeats, divisions, and elongations in notation.

3. You and students together arbitrarily identify rhythm patterns of two or four underlying macrobeats in length. Beams in notation are usually good guides for making selections, and choices need not coincide with what you might have decided are tonal patterns.

4. You and students together read by chanting each rhythm pattern one at a time using beat-function rhythm syllables. Separate rhythm patterns and take a deep breath before each is performed. Be certain all durations are chanted on the same pitch, but with inflections corresponding to expression, so as not to convey keyality or tonality.

5. Soon after students understand the logic of how beat-function rhythm syllables are associated with notation on the staff, guide them in identifying by themselves remaining rhythm patterns. Individual students take turns in selecting rhythm patterns for the class to read in ensemble.

6. Unlike with tonal patterns, now the class reads all rhythm patterns in the melody continuously from beginning to end using beat-function rhythm syllables. However, deep breaths are taken appropriately. There are no pauses between chanting of rhythm patterns. To do otherwise would distort tempo.

7. Conduct students as they read and perform instrumentally all rhythm patterns in the melody continuously from beginning to end, breathing with artistic phrasing. All durations are performed on the same pitch with musical inflections, typically B♭ concert, so as not to indicate keyality or tonality. Emphasize, for the further development of students' musicianship, importance of audiating and associating beat-function rhythm syllables with durations when reading and not habitually reciting or thinking note-value names.

Melodic Patterns

1. Explain to students melodic patterns combine tonal patterns and rhythm patterns, and soon, with proper preparation, they will be reading melodic patterns.

2. After you establish meter and tempo, students look at the notation of a familiar or unfamiliar short melody. Ask them to scan the melody and subjectively identify and audiate rhythm patterns in the melody by using beat-function rhythm syllables. That is, they only audiate, not perform, rhythm patterns.

3. After you establish tonality and keyality, and beginning pitch if necessary, students look at the notation of the same melody. Ask them to scan the melody and subjectively identify and audiate tonal patterns in the melody by using movable-*do* syllables. That is, they only audiate, not perform, the tonal patterns.

4. Now, without attempting to explain how tonal patterns and rhythm patterns are combined into melodic patterns in audiation, ask them to notationally audiate (read silently and not sing or chant) the melody, observing both tonal and rhythmic components simultaneously. As of yet, research does not explain the process of how melodic patterns are audiated. What is known is individuals have unique ways of defining and objectifying melodic patterns.

5. Giving students a few minutes to audiate the melody, ask them to read and perform vocally the melody in entirety using one or more neutral syllables or the text of the song. Neither tonal syllables nor rhythm syllables are to be performed when reading melodic patterns, only audiated in a way each student finds comfortable.

6. After you have notated parts to accommodate transpositions and ranges of instruments in the ensemble, conduct students as they read in unison and perform instrumentally the melody from beginning to end. You might tell students it is natural to unconsciously maintain in audiation tonal syllables and rhythm

syllables as they are reading notation. Syllables are brought into consciousness when needed.

7. If students are not already astonished by realizing by themselves they now can truly read music notation and there is no longer a need for them to perfunctorily decode symbols, alert them to the fact audiation is primarily responsible for improving their musicianship. True, a scant few may have already been able to hear the sound of music notation without consulting a music instrument, but in all probability they were achieving that in a boring and mechanical rather than artistic manner. Underscore notational audiation is one advantage of having learned to use tonal syllables and rhythm syllables. Other benefits to be acquired will be development of their abilities to improvise and create music. Although unlikely, expect a few students not to be motivated to continue participating in learning sequence activities. Little more can be done for them. It is a pity they are bereft of imagination and that anticipation of acquiring those inspiring skills does not fascinate them.

Improvisation

Musicians engage in improvisation in various ways. Probably oldest is melodic variation. An intact melody is embellished primarily tonally and to some extent rhythmically without disrupting the thread of melody. Next is a second part functioning as harmony. Closely related is an obbligato and ostinato, and akin to those is improvising continuous rhythm patterns void of melody. A somewhat different type of improvisation takes place when an artist performs music in diversified styles of well-known composers. Some composers notate music requiring performers to improvise within restrictions found in the notation and/or freely depending upon what other musicians in ensemble have performed or are performing. Then there are musicians who improvise as guided by figured bass or chord symbols in notation. With regard to the latter, unfortunately inexperienced musicians rely on scales rather than harmonic progressions to direct their performance. Finally, the peak is harmonic improvisation, and it includes two types: Improvising a melody to on-going harmonic progressions and improvising harmonic progressions to an on-going melody.

Improvising a melody over harmonic progressions is more complex than improvising a melodic variation. Rather than simply embellishing a melody, a melody is changed in improvisation in accordance with anticipation of forthcoming harmonic progressions as it simultaneously and artistically embodies select motifs of the original melody. In a word, it foretells and leads into one or more subsequent harmonic possibilities. For information to supplement and expand the following outlined procedures for teaching harmonic improvisation and composition, read my books, *Improvisation in the Music Classroom* and *Harmonic Improvisation for Adult Musicians*. Both are listed in the Bibliography.

Because students are knowledgeable about tonal syllables and rhythm syllables, the transition from notational audiation to audiation for harmonic improvisation is accomplished with ease. Rather than performing syllabic tonal patterns as arpeggios, now all pitches in the arpeggio are performed as a chord (literally, a triad). Notated below are two harmonic progressions, each comprising three chords in major tonality. The first includes tonic, dominant-seventh, tonic. The second includes tonic, subdominant, tonic. On the following page are two harmonic progressions, each similarly comprising three chords in harmonic minor tonality. Roman numerals and tonal syllables are indicated under each chord in the harmonic progressions.

Major Tonality

Harmonic Minor Tonality

Major Tonality and Usual Duple Meter

1. Ask students to audiate eight macrobeats in usual duple meter. Then you and students individually and/or in ensemble perform a series of rhythm patterns superimposed on the eight underlying macrobeats using one or more neutral syllables. Macro/microbeat and division patterns are best, but all other functions may be used.

2. Divide the class into three sections. Each section sings one of the pitches in the tonic chord in major tonality using movable-*do* syllables. Adhering to voice leadings in the notated harmonic progressions, follow the same procedure for the dominant-seventh chord. When that is satisfactorily accomplished, students quietly sing the tonic, dominant-seventh, tonic progression humming or using one or more neutral syllables. The progression is based on eight underlying macrobeats. As notated, the tonic chord is sung for the first-four underlying macrobeats, the dominant-seventh chord for the next two underlying macrobeats, and the tonic chord for the last two underlying macrobeats.

3. As the class sings repetitions of the harmonic progression, students take turns improvising a melody over the harmonic progression. Only the three pitches constituting the chord being sung but any rhythm pattern functions may be used in the improvisation. Non-harmonic tones are not included at this

time. Until students develop self-confidence in improvising solo, several students may initially improvise at the same time.

4. After explaining transpositions, if necessary, and assigning pitches to be played on each instrument so all are performing in major tonality and B♭ concert keyality (for brass and woodwinds) or major tonality and D concert keyality (for strings), individual students take turns performing improvisations based on the same harmonic progression on their instruments as the remainder of the students perform on their instruments the chords in the harmonic progression.

5. Follow the same procedure outlined in steps 1, 2, 3, and 4 above replacing the dominant-seventh chord with the subdominant chord. As notated below, the tonic chord is sung for the first-four underlying macrobeats, the subdominant chord for the next two underlying macrobeats, and the tonic chord for the last two underlying macrobeats.

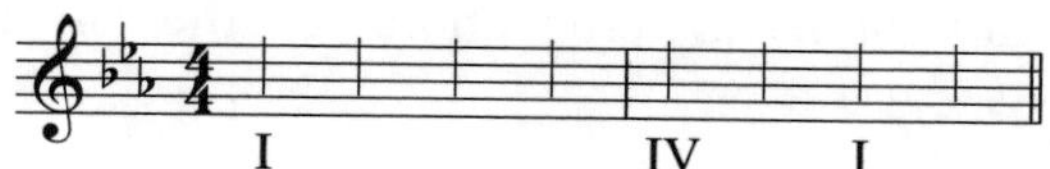

6. Following the same procedure outlined in steps 1, 2, 3, and 4, now all three chords are included in the harmonic progression. As notated, the tonic chord is sung for the first-two underlying macrobeats, the subdominant chord for the next two underlying macrobeats, the dominant-seventh chord for the next two underlying macrobeats, and the tonic chord for the last two macrobeats.

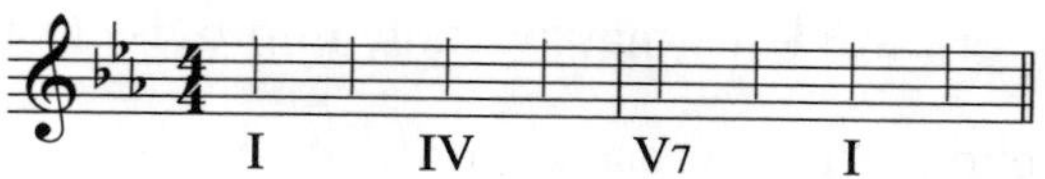

HARMONIC MINOR TONALITY AND USUAL DUPLE METER

1. Ask students to audiate eight macrobeats in usual duple meter. Then you and students individually and/or in ensemble perform a series of rhythm patterns superimposed on eight underlying macrobeats using one or more neutral syllables. Macro/microbeat and division patterns are best, but other functions may be used.

2. Divide the class into three sections. Each section sings one of the pitches in the tonic chord in harmonic minor tonality using movable-*do* syllables. Adhering to the voice leadings in the notated harmonic progressions, follow the same procedure for the dominant-seventh chord. When that is satisfactorily accomplished, students quietly sing the tonic, dominant-seventh, tonic progression humming or using one or more neutral syllables. The progression is based on eight underlying macrobeats. As notated, the tonic chord is sung for the first-four underlying macrobeats, the dominant-seventh chord for the next two underlying macrobeats, and the tonic chord for the last two underlying macrobeats.

3. As the class sings repetitions of the harmonic progression, students take turns improvising a melody over the harmonic progression. Only the three pitches constituting the chord being sung but any rhythm pattern functions may be used in the improvisation. Non-harmonic tones are not included at this time. Until students develop self-confidence in improvising solo, several students may initially improvise at the same time.

4. After explaining transpositions, if necessary, and assigning pitches to be played on each instrument so all are performing in harmonic minor tonality and G concert keyality (for brass, woodwind, and strings) individual students take turns performing improvisations based on the same harmonic

progression on their instruments as the remainder of the students perform the chords in the harmonic progression.

5. Follow the same procedure outlined in steps 1, 2, 3, and 4 replacing the dominant-seventh chord with the subdominant chord. As notated, the tonic chord is sung for the first-four underlying macrobeats, the subdominant chord for the next two underlying macrobeats, and the tonic chord for the last two underlying macrobeats.

6. Following the same procedure outlined in steps 1, 2, 3, and 4, now all three chords are included in the harmonic progression. As notated below, the tonic chord is sung for the first-two underlying macrobeats, the subdominant chord for the next two underlying macrobeats, the dominant-seventh chord for the next two underlying macrobeats, and the tonic chord for the last two underlying macrobeats.

Major Tonality and Usual Triple Meter

1. Ask students to audiate eight macrobeats in usual triple meter. Then you and students individually and/or in ensemble perform a series of rhythm patterns superimposed on eight underlying macrobeats using one or more neutral syllables. Macro/microbeat and division patterns are best, but other functions may also be used.

2. Divide the class into three sections. Each section sings one of the pitches in the tonic chord in major tonality using tonal syllables. Adhering to the voice leadings in the notated harmonic

progressions, follow the same procedure for the dominant-seventh chord. When that is satisfactorily accomplished, students quietly sing the tonic, dominant-seventh, tonic progression humming or using one or more neutral syllables. The progression is based on eight underlying macrobeats. As notated, the tonic chord is sung for the first-four underlying macrobeats, the dominant-seventh chord for the next two underlying macrobeats, and the tonic chord for the last two underlying macrobeats.

3. As the class sings repetitions of the harmonic progression, students take turns improvising a melody over the harmonic progression. Only the three pitches constituting the chord being sung but any rhythm pattern functions may be used in the improvisation. Non-harmonic tones are not included at this time. Until students develop self-confidence in improvising solo, several students may initially improvise at the same time.

4. After explaining transpositions, if necessary, and assigning pitches to be played on each instrument so all are performing in major tonality and B♭ concert keyality (for brass and woodwinds) or major tonality and D keyality (for strings), individual students take turns performing improvisations based on the same harmonic progression on their instruments as the remainder of the students perform the chords in the harmonic progression on their instruments.

5. Follow the same procedure outlined in steps 1, 2, 3, and 4 replacing the dominant-seventh chord with the subdominant chord. As notated, the tonic chord is sung for the first-four underlying macrobeats, the subdominant chord for the next two underlying macrobeats, and the tonic chord for the last two underlying macrobeats.

6. Following the same procedure outlined in steps 1, 2, 3, and 4, now all three chords are included in the harmonic progression. As notated, the tonic chord is sung for the first-two underlying macrobeats, the subdominant chord for the next two underlying macrobeats, the dominant-seventh chord for the next two underlying macrobeats, and the tonic chord for the last two underlying macrobeats.

Harmonic Minor Tonality and Usual Triple Meter

1. Ask students to audiate eight macrobeats in usual triple meter. Then you and students individually and/or in ensemble perform a series of rhythm patterns superimposed on eight underlying macrobeats using one or more neutral syllables. Macro/microbeat and division patterns are best, but other functions may also be used.

2. Divide the class into three sections. Each section sings one of the pitches in the tonic chord in harmonic minor tonality using movable-*do* syllables. Adhering to the voice leadings in the notated harmonic progressions, follow the same procedure for the dominant-seventh chord. When that is satisfactorily accomplished, students quietly sing the tonic, dominant-seventh, tonic progression humming or using one or more neutral syllables. The progression is based on eight underlying macrobeats. As notated, the tonic chord is sung for the first-four underlying macrobeats, the dominant-seventh chord for the next two underlying macrobeats, and the tonic chord for the last two underlying macrobeats.

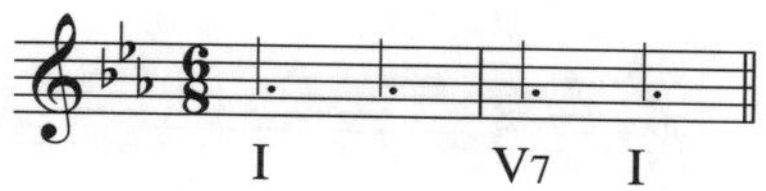

3. As the class sings repetitions of the harmonic progression, students take turns improvising a melody over the harmonic progression. Only the three pitches constituting the chord being sung but any rhythm pattern functions may be used in the improvisation. Non-harmonic tones are not included at this time. Until students develop self-confidence in improvising solo, several students may initially improvise at the same time.

4. After explaining transpositions, if necessary, and assigning pitches to be played on each instrument so all are performing in harmonic minor tonality and G concert keyality (for brass, woodwind, and strings) individual students take turns performing improvisations based on the same harmonic progression on their instruments as the remainder of the students perform the chords in the harmonic progression on their instruments.

5. Follow the same procedure outlined in steps 1, 2, 3, and 4 above replacing the dominant-seventh chord with the subdominant chord. As notated, the tonic chord is sung for the first-four underlying macrobeats, the subdominant chord for the next two underlying macrobeats, and the tonic chord for the last two underlying macrobeats.

6. Following the same procedure outlined in steps 1, 2, 3, and 4, now all three chords are included in the harmonic progression. As notated, the tonic chord is sung for the first-two underlying macrobeats, the subdominant chord for the next two underlying macrobeats, the dominant-seventh chord for the next two underlying macrobeats, and the tonic chord for the last two underlying macrobeats.

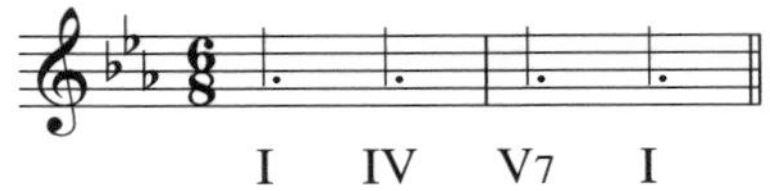

Advanced Improvisation

1. Now that students are facile in improvising using only those pitches in a given chord, they should find it desirable and challenging to include non-harmonic pitches in longer improvisations, including various arrangements of tonic, subdominant, and dominant-seventh chords superimposed perhaps on sixteen underlying macrobeats. Passing tones, such as C and E♭ (*re* and *fa*) in a B♭ chord in major tonality, are initially easiest. Also, additional keyalities in major and harmonic minor tonalities may be contemplated.

2. As introduction to the fulfillment of possibilities for instrumental improvisation, students are introduced to additional chords in major tonality commonly found in standard types and styles of music. The three most consequential among them are the supertonic-seventh (II7), submediant-seventh (VI7), and mediant-seventh (III7). They are notated below with Roman numerals and movable-*do* syllables. The voice leadings are compatible when sung and/or played in conjunction with the tonic, dominant-seventh, and subdominant chords. As before, students are asked to sing harmonic progressions including one or more of the additional chords before they are played instrumentally.

3. By this time, students should be performing instrumental improvisations with reasonably confidence. That being the case and in preparation for their improvisations in standard types of music, such as jazz, letter-name chord symbols corresponding to Roman numerals are explained. For example, in major tonality and C keyality, the chord symbol C is the I chord; G7, the V7 chord; and F, the IV chord. They should anticipate seeing letter-name chord symbols in professional music notation.

4. It will be noticed the II7, VI7, and III7 are major chords, and they are found particularly in folk, country, and blue grass music as well as ragtime and early jazz. However, with the introduction of more contemporary styles of jazz, these so called major-minor seventh chords were often supplemented with minor-minor seventh chords (*D F A C* for II7 and A C *E* G for VI7). These two chords are almost a mainstay in jazz improvisations, especially in turnarounds (transitions from A to B parts and vice versa in popular songs. Thus, students who desire to participate in extended improvisations should become comfortable with singing and playing these chords.

5. Finally, as time permits, additional tonalities, such as Dorian and Mixolydian, and additional meters, typically written using the measure signatures 5/4 and 7/4, might be explored. For guidance in introducing these and other tonalities and meters, read my book, *Learning Sequences in Music: A Contemporary Music Learning Theory*.

Creative Composition

There are two components to notational audiation in learning sequence activities: reading and writing. Students have already achieved in reading music notation by audiating tonal and rhythm syllables. Now they can use that information and those skills to write their own compositions.

1. After distributing blank staff paper, ask students to insert the measure signature 4/4 and the *do* signature of two flats. (*Jump Right In: The Instrumental Series* composition books may be used.) Of course, you may substitute another usual duple measure signature and/or *do* signature to be used with major tonality. Direct students to mark off eight blank measures using bar lines, allowing sufficient space in each measure to accommodate whatever they may choose to compose. You may indicate on your own sheet of staff paper or at the board how all this is notated.

2. Show students how to indicate one letter-name chord symbol or Roman numeral above each of the eight measures. For example, the harmonic progression might be **B♭**, **E♭**, F7, **B♭**, **E♭**, **B♭**, F7, **B♭** or I , IV, V7, I, IV, I, V7, I.

3. Establish D keyality in major tonality and usual duple meter.

4. Audiating whatever rhythm patterns they choose, ask students to create in audiation a melody covering the eight measures and then, as they please, to notate it one measure at a time or all at once. Chord pitches and non-harmonic tones may be used in accordance with the harmonic progression.

5. Volunteers may sing their melodies for the class as other students sing the harmonic progression. They also listen critically and offer comments.

6. Assist students in transposing their instrumental parts as necessary. Volunteers may perform their melodies for the class as other students perform the harmonic progression on their instruments. They also listen critically and offer comments.

7. As time permits, students may compose another composition using another harmonic progression of their choice. There may be more than one chord in a measure, including II7, VI7, and/or III7 along with I, IV, and V7. They decide the length and keyality of the composition in major tonality and usual duple meter. As before, compositions may be sung or played.

8. Follow the same procedure for creating compositions in harmonic minor tonality, using only I, V7, and IV and/or usual triple meter.

9. The pinnacle of this activity is encouraging students to notate arrangements of their compositions for various instrumental ensembles. With their developed skills in audiating movable-*do* syllables and notational audiation, transpositions should be well understood and easy to accomplish.

Ancillary Concepts

In addition to the foregoing, there are other untold advantages to introducing music learning theory and learning sequence activities to students. How some of these benefits may be considered in practical application is outlined below.

1. In rehearsals, band members sing an harmonic progression of tonic, dominant-seventh, tonic chords in B♭ concert keyality and major tonality. Immediately after, all students quietly hum the tonic pitch of B♭. Then they audiate and play B♭ concert in unison on their instruments. By comparing what they are audiating with the sound coming from their instrument, they adjust and tune their instrument by themselves. The same procedure is followed at the onset of orchestra rehearsals. The only difference is the keyality is D and tonality is harmonic minor. No longer is there necessity of students consulting electronic instruments or constantly seeking your assistance.

2. Given a background in music learning theory and learning sequence activities, students are able to participate in small ensembles in and out of school with minimal guidance. As a result of performing an assortment of types and styles of music, many components of their musicianship are enhanced, primarily their intonation and sense of tempo. Perhaps most important is participation in small ensembles where students have an opportunity to experiment with improvisation and hear their compositions and instrumental arrangements performed.

3. Competence in audiating major and harmonic minor tonalities and usual duple, triple, and combined meters provides the foundation for audiating other tonalities and meters. With little instruction from you, students should be able to explore differences in Dorian and Mixolydian tonalities as compared to major and harmonic minor tonalities. Also, consequential attention to macrobeats of unequal temporal length in unusual meters, commonly notated in 5/4 and 7/4, compared to macrobeats of equal

temporal length in usual meters, will broaden their abilities to read, write, and perform music comprehensively.

A productive way students might acquire competence in audiating and performing unfamiliar tonalities and meters is to learn to play a music instrument they have not played before by using a student book and CD from *Jump Right In: The Instrumental Series*. It would be best if brass or woodwind players instruct themselves on a string instrument, and vice versa. This activity offers percussion players a superb opportunity to become acquainted with melody instruments.

4. Rather than the band or orchestra mounting a public performance in common fashion, occasionally it might be worthwhile to inform parents, school administrators, and other interested persons about what has been taking place during rehearsal time in terms of learning sequence activities. Most onlookers will be astounded by capabilities students demonstrate. In addition to improvisations, the ensemble may perform individual students' compositions and arrangements.

5. If students are not already aware of their musical growth as a result of investing time in learning sequence activities, guide them through a before and after scenario. It should prove gratifying to you as well as students to remind them of skills they have acquired in audiation, notational audiation, improvisation, and creativity. Perhaps a desirable outcome not obvious to them is they have learned to listen to, not simply to hear, their own performance and that of others at the same time.

Part 4

Introducing Middle and High School Choral and Classroom Music Students to Learning Sequence Activities

There are probably as many ways to teach elementary and middle school classroom music as there are teachers who do that teaching. Though the following is somewhat redundant of information in the Introduction but requires emphasis, rarely is there a practical and workable document to guide elementary and middle school classroom music teachers in systematically offering students a sequential music curriculum to serve as readiness for advanced music instruction and participation. No doubt there are teachers who do a creditable job of acculturating students to attributes of music, but if skills and practical knowledge are taught, rarely are they sequential within a semester or academic year. Worse, even if such sequential instruction were a reality, expectation of pedagogy being sequential from one academic year to the next, even with the same music teacher, would be extraordinary. Not only do music teachers differ in subjective methodologies, arbitrary schedules and administrative practices often preclude the eventuality of establishing a building-wide or system-wide objective music curriculum. Unfortunately, entertainment haphazardly supercedes education in the minds of many administrators, and because they are woefully uninformed, so too the former looms large in the minds of many classroom music teachers and choral directors. It is not uncommon for fine-arts teachers to declare an imposed curriculum, including a democratically established one, would stifle their personal freedom and creativity. Such an unlikely outcome notwithstanding, a purview of our immediate environment attests to the obligatory retribution students remit under current circumstances as a result of not being exposed to a viable sequential music curriculum. Lyrics, histrionics, gimmickry, and electronic and visual aids are presumed to be satisfactory substitutes for audiating, listening to, and performing undistorted music in a sensitive manner.

The purpose of Part 4 is to offer you, the middle and high school choral director and classroom music teacher, guidance in developing musicianship of students who previously have not received an adequate music education. That is not to suggest remedial instruction is possible. It is not, but compensatory instruction is feasible. Students learn to audiate best when they are young, the younger the better. What has been lost cannot be recaptured. That is why I have devoted so many professional years to early childhood music teaching, often acculturating groups of newborns and young children while at the same time engaging in corresponding observational and empirical research. A realistic approach to counteracting effects of older students' deficits is to introduce them to learning sequence activities based on music learning theory.

With exception of a paucity of select ensembles, it is no secret an outlandish number of students who participate in classroom singing, performance ensembles, and adult choral groups cannot read music notation. At best, they may simply name notes and define other signs and symbols bereft of audiation, typically encouraged to learn by imitation or worse yet, by rote. The situation is unconscionable if for no other reason than it can be ameliorated with desire and effort on the part of participants, classroom music teachers, and choral directors. Moreover, when observed under objective conditions, most students cannot sing or are otherwise unaware of the tonic (resting tone) of music they are performing or have just finished performing.

Perhaps that is one of the causes of poor intonation and why so many singers are dependent on instrumental accompaniment to learn and perform compositions in preparation for public appearances. Often rigid choreographic activity is rehearsed to mask poor musicianship. And, it should not go unmentioned the great majority of students, including those in advanced choral organizations, are unable to improvise or document in music notation melodies they might wish to compose. Harmonization without consulting music notation is believed to be something only few privileged ones can enjoy. Fortunately, given appropriate guidance and instruction, most if not all of these disorders can be obviated. The following outlined suggestions in terms of learning sequence activities are intended for you to assist students in learning how to audiate. The value of acquiring knowledge and audiation is untold and compelling.

Transitional Preparation

Part 1, *Movement and Interactive Breathing as Readiness for Learning Rhythm*, includes relevant information for teaching students of all ages who are engaged in instrumental, choral, and classroom music. On the other hand, information in Part 3, *Learning Sequence Activities for Middle and High School Instrumental Students*, is specifically for instrumental teachers and students. I recommend Part 1 be read prudently for definitions and explanations, and to embellish and reinforce many pedagogical suggestions proffered here in Part 4. I am aware some pedagogical suggestions accompanying the twenty-four melodies intended to encourage students to participate in free-flowing continuous movement may not be attractive to adolescents. Nonetheless, because experiencing space before musical time is essential for grasping a sense of rhythm, I urge you to muster ingenuity and maturity to dissipate initial diffidence of students, particularly young men. I have suggested techniques in that regard in Part 1 for young students, but additional ones will be offered herein. Although not all concepts presented for teaching instrumental music parallel those for teaching choral and classroom music, you might at least scan Part 3.

Results of a music aptitude test will serve you in garnering valuable knowledge about students you will be teaching. Either the *Musical Aptitude Profile* or *Advanced Measures of Music Audiation* is recommended for administration. Information pertaining to these and other tests may be found in *Introduction to Research and the Psychology of Music* and *Music Aptitude and Related Tests* (G-5719), a brochure published by GIA offered free of charge. Both are mine and are listed in the Bibliography. Test results will guide you in teaching to individual musical differences among students. When students' individual musical needs are taken into account, those with limited potential will not become frustrated and others with exceptional potential will not become bored. You will discover reading test manuals and ancillary books about interpretation and use of music aptitude test results to be rewarding.

Outlined below are general issues to reflect on for thoughtfully presenting instruction based on music learning theory and learning sequence activities to students who have been taught music conventionally. It is expected you will necessarily contribute other important topics not specifically addressed herein but are uniquely suited to you and your students. Specifically, it is well to keep in mind students who have been subjected to scribble, and know they have, will undoubtedly bring along with them poor attitudes toward school music, not always popular music, when they enter upper grades. Many have been conditioned to look upon music classes with disinterest and music teachers with disrespect. Thus, you must be tolerant and patient, and without agreeing or sympathizing with students, let it be known you understand what their thoughts might be. Given the magnetic qualities of learning sequence activities coupled with knowledgeable and caring teachers, students soon become intrigued with understanding and participating in music in a functional manner. Once over the struggle, you will find teaching more enjoyable if for no other reason you can communicate with students as musicians without resorting to unsubstantiated and senseless metaphors and euphemisms. Success is definitely possible but not necessarily immediate.

Explain to students you are interested in spending time with them to investigate benefits of a new approach to learning music. You believe it will broaden them musically by increasing their skills and knowledge. However, to achieve the goal, you will need their cooperation and assistance. They can help by listening carefully, being open-minded and patient with themselves, and offering you astute positive criticism. You will arrange sessions for interaction of your and their ideas, but they must remember progress in their musicianship may not be instantaneous.

By learning to audiate, they will be able to look at music notation and hear it in their minds before playing it on an instrument. In that way, by audiating what they are going to play before they play it, music notation can be translated into performance with superior intonation and rhythm in the choir and classroom. Further, audiation is the basis of improvisation and composition. If you and they are successful in this new endeavor, in addition to participating in large school ensembles, they will be capable of participating in small groups and performing various types of popular music without aid of music notation. In time students may compose and arrange music they and others will enjoy performing.

An entire period is not directed toward learning sequence activities. In the beginning, perhaps ten minutes or so, preferably at the onset or end of each period, might be appropriate. That is, do not attempt an abrupt total alteration of methodology. The change from common-practice schooling to current research-based instruction must be gradual over a series of learning sequence activity sessions. Both types of teaching are undertaken simultaneously. Initially, traditional activities will assume the majority of time. Once students realize the practicality and value of music learning theory and learning sequence activities, the majority of time will naturally be magnetized to those concepts. A new world of possibilities for making music will inspire students. They will be captured by endless potentialities. Soon students will intuit their newly acquired abilities to audiate and improvise, amid other bonuses, will improve their ability to read and write music notation.

As will be discovered, the cornerstone of learning sequence activities is development of tonal and rhythm pattern vocabularies following the procedures outlined in the *Reference Handbook for Using Learning Sequence Activities*. Regular choral and classroom activities follow the few minutes dedicated to learning sequence activities at the beginning of a class.

Pedagogy

Rhythm Development

1. Though harmonic improvisation may need to be sacrificed, perhaps a more practical and acceptable approach with some older choral students and those enrolled in classroom music might be to begin with rhythm rather than tonal components of learning sequence activities. Because so many male adolescents did not sing using a singing voice quality before or during their voice change, they are too embarrassed to attempt to sing, and if they were to try, most would now find it tolerantly impossible to use a singing voice quality. To suggest or ask them to sing makes them defensive and more alienated from music. That is an important reason for beginning instruction with rhythm. As students are progressing in rhythm activities, take every apropos occasion to remind them how their motivation to participate in learning sequence activities has increased their musicianship and created prospects for alternative performance opportunities.

2. As emphasized throughout the book, ability to engage in continuous free-flowing movement is fundamental to acquiring physical coordination, and physical coordination provides the wherewithal to perform rhythmically in a relaxed and artistic manner. Environmental and psychological conditions permitting, all students, regardless of chronological age, benefit from being guided in movement activities. Moreover, advocate activities are movement in space before movement in musical time, the latter, when experienced out of sequence, is being rigidly preoccupied with consistent tempo and in striving for accuracy in relationships among note values. Because it is well

understood convincing older students to participate in spatial movement is not easy when attempted conventionally, described below are unconventional techniques I have found to be appealing to adolescents. If students stubbornly refuse to participate, it would not be wise to insist. Psychological harm is more detrimental than omitting important steps in sequential learning. Of course, with omissions students' rhythm achievement will be limited, but some accomplishment is feasible without first acquiring the experience of free-flowing and relaxed continuous movement in space. Nonetheless, most students will eventually realize mutual cooperation is valuable for their musical development. Grasp the moment, because though they are not learning in a sequential manner, spatial movement at any time contributes to overall music achievement.

Movement, Breathing and Coordination

3. A reexamination of the first few paragraphs in Part 1 will provide you with a clear rationale for the importance of space over musical time. Also, a review of the second-last paragraph before Melody 1 in Overview of the Melodies in Part 1 will refresh your memory about relevant games for younger students that might apply to some older students you are teaching. Ongoing team scores may be kept and/or prizes awarded for the following games.

4. Ask students one at a time to move any or all parts of their body without speaking or using lips or tongue to suggest how he or she is thinking of an uncommon pronunciation of his or her name. Movement must be sustained and free-flowing within and/or between body parts. That is, if different parts of the body are used, transition from one part to the other must be continuous, without pauses. Encourage use of legs, feet, hands, fingers, and deep breathing. The student whispers to you how the name is to be pronounced. Within time limits, classmates guess at the pronunciation and you decide who made the best guess. If

free-flowing continuous movement is interrupted, the leader is required to announce the veiled pronunciation and the next student takes a turn.

5. Ask students one at a time to move any or all parts of their body without speaking or using lips or tongue to give directions to another student. It may be suggested the respondent stand, be seated, open a window, adjust a shade, open a door, find a specific book, and so on. Movement must be sustained and free-flowing within and/or between body parts. That is, if different parts of the body are used, transition from one part to the other must be continuous, without pauses. Encourage use of legs, feet, hands, fingers, and deep breathing. Students are given a set time to correctly determine what he or she is to do.

6. Ask students one at a time to move any or all parts of their body without speaking or using lips or tongue to indicate to another student what he or she is thinking. Some verbal clues may be given before physical motion is undertaken. Movement must be sustained and free-flowing within and/or between body parts. That is, if different parts of the body are used, transition from one part to the other must be continuous, without any pauses. Encourage use of legs, feet, hands, fingers, and deep breathing. Students are given a set time to correctly determine the thought.

7. Two students engage in a pantomime. One is pitcher and the other batter in a baseball game. Always in action of continuous free-flowing movement and deep breathing, the pitcher throws the invisible ball and the batter swings at the ball and hits it at what you, as umpire, is anticipated to be the appropriate time. Three inappropriate swings and both the pitcher and batter are disqualified and another team takes a turn. It is important that after the ball is thrown and hit, both players sustain continuous free-flowing movement. If either of the pair interrupts or ceases movement at any time, the two forfeit the game for their team.

8. Two students engage in a pantomime. One is quarterback and the other receiver in a football game. Always in action of continuous free-flowing movement and deep breathing, the quarterback throws the invisible football and the receiver catches it at what you, as referee or umpire, is anticipated to be the appropriate time. After three failures, another quarterback and receiver take a turn. Again, after the football is thrown and caught, both players sustain continuous free-flowing movement. If either of the pair interrupts or ceases movement, the two forfeit the game for their team.

9. During and after involving students in movement activities, I suggest you assist them in becoming physically coordinated. Most will require guidance in this endeavor. How well they are coordinated will affect their rhythm development. Rather than repeating here recommended steps for consummating physical coordination, it should suffice for you to review pedagogical suggestions 3 and 4 for Melody 21 in Part 1. Though it is a compromise, do not consider all eleven outlined sequential steps to be mandatory. Whatever you can accomplish will prove worthwhile. However, if class time is a premium, it would be better to limit time devoted to each step so as to complete the entire segued series in a few minutes than to strive for perfection for any one.

   Before moving on to further pedagogical suggestions, a momentary digression of brief explanations of rhythm concepts based on music learning theory and their practical application to learning sequence activities might be necessary. If deemed not, please skip to suggestion 10.

Macrobeats, Microbeats, and Rhythm Patterns

Three elements that define rhythm in both usual and unusual meters are macrobeats, microbeats, and rhythm patterns. Macrobeats are fundamental to microbeats and rhythm patterns, because microbeats and rhythm patterns are superimposed on macrobeats in audiation. Microbeats are shorter than macrobeats and are derived from equal division of macrobeats. When macrobeats are divided into two microbeats of equal length, the result is usual duple meter. When macrobeats are divided into three microbeats of equal length, the result is usual triple meter. When some macrobeats are divided into two microbeats of equal length and other macrobeats are divided into three microbeats of equal but shorter length than the two microbeats, regardless of the sequence of groupings, the result is usual combined meter. In usual meter all macrobeats (for example, quarter notes in 2/4) are of equal length. When macrobeats are not of equal length (for example, half notes and dotted-half notes in 5/4), music is in unusual meter. Macrobeats in unusual meter include two or three microbeats, all of the same equal length. When macrobeats are grouped in twos in a rhythm pattern, meter is unusual paired meter. When macrobeats are grouped in threes in a rhythm pattern, meter is unusual unpaired meter.

Rhythm comprises a series of rhythm patterns audiated concurrently with underlying macrobeats and microbeats. There are seven functions of rhythm patterns: Macro/microbeats, divisions, elongation, division/elongations, rests, ties, and upbeats. The functions may be viewed in notation in Part 3 under Rhythm Development. Most common rhythm patterns in usual duple and triple meters are notated in Part 1, Melody 23, suggestion 3. For a comprehensive discussion of rhythm, see my book, *Rhythm: Contrasting the Implications of Audiation and Notation*. The book is listed in the Bibliography. Immediate and concise definitions are included in the Glossary.

Measure Signatures

Simple duple, compound duple, simple triple, and compound triple, terms declared by music theorists to describe measure signatures, are often used to explain meter. Students are taught meter of music is determined by number of beats in a measure, indicated by measure signatures. How macrobeats are divided is ignored. For example, students learn music in 2/4 is simple duple meter, duple because there are two beats (quarter notes) in a measure and simple because each beat is divided into two beats (eighth notes). They are taught only twos need be considered, and there is no attempt to distinguish between types of beats. Likewise students learn music in 6/8 is compound duple meter; duple meter because there are two beats (dotted-quarter notes) in a measure and compound because each beat is divided into three beats (eighth notes). They are taught both twos and threes need to be considered. Not grasped is duple and triple can be audiated and demonstrated in movement, but simple and compound cannot because their meanings hinge entirely on arithmetic associated with notation of measure signatures.

Students are taught music in 3/4 is in simple triple meter; triple because there are three beats (quarter notes) in a measure and simple because each beat is divided into two beats (eighth notes). It is called simple even though both twos and threes need to be considered. This inconsistency partially results from the mistaken belief note values indicate whether a note functions as a macrobeat or microbeat. However, note values do not indicate types of beats. For example, a quarter note may be a macrobeat and an eighth note a microbeat in 2/4, a dotted-quarter note may be a macrobeat and an eighth note a microbeat in 6/8, and a dotted-whole note may be a macrobeat and a half note a microbeat in 6/4. When macrobeats are audiated in terms of weight rather than accents, meter underlying two measures of 3/4 is audiated the same way as meter underlying one measure of 6/8. Both are usual triple meter. Just as two key signatures can be enharmonic, so two measure signatures, such as 3/4 and 6/8, can be enrhythmic.

Music written in 9/8 is commonly said to be in compound triple meter; triple because there are three beats (dotted-quarter notes) in a measure and compound because each beat is divided into three beats (eighth notes). It is called compound even though only threes need to be considered, but again, that inconsistency is routinely overlooked. It is important to recognize in 9/8, three dotted-quarter notes together equal one macrobeat, because a dotted-quarter note represents a microbeat, not a macrobeat, and eighth notes represent divisions of microbeats. One measure of nine eighth-notes in 9/8 is audiated as if it were written as one measure of 3/4 written with three eighth-note triplets, or as half a measure of 6/8 written with three sixteenth-note triplets. All three measure signatures (9/8, 3/4, and 6/8) may be, and usually are, enrhythmic. They all typically represent usual triple meter.

To complicate the problem, young students are often taught music written in 4/4 is simple quadruple, and music written in 12/8 is compound quadruple. Unfortunately, this implies a difference between music written in 2/4 and 4/4 and between music written in 6/8 and 12/8. Music written using one measure of 4/4 is usually audiated as either two measures of 2/4 or as one measure of 2/2, all being usual duple meter. Similarly, music written using one measure of 12/8 is usually audiated as two measures of 6/8, both being usual triple meter.

Rhythm Syllables

In transition from conventional instruction to learning sequence activities and notational audiation, students begin to explore use of rhythm syllables to read and write rhythm notation. Rhythm syllables are also of enormous benefit in learning to improvise and compose music. The recommended rhythm syllables are based on beat functions, not time-value names, of notes. Rationale of the syllables is found in Part 1, Melody 23, suggestion 4. Following suggestion 7 for Melody 23 is a description of rhythm syllables corresponding to notation. Take whatever time is necessary not to memorize but to familiarize yourself with the syllables. As you use them in your teaching, your natural comfort in chanting them will become increasingly evident. You will find students' acceptance of them and how quickly they learn to be astounding as well as impressive.

Establishing Consistency of Tempo

10. Assuming students have physically moved in space apart from time, they are ready to superimpose musical time on space. It is accomplished by flicking wrists while upper parts of the body, particularly arms, are in free-flowing continuous movement. Clapping is unconditionally avoided. It is imperative students initially remain nonlocomotive. If it can be accomplished without students being embarrassed and self-consciousness, moving in locomotive space may be undertaken in association with flicking wrists and sweeping arms. The purpose of flicking wrists on macrobeats as arms are continuously and freely moving is to audiate space. The physical distance in space between flicking of wrists on one macrobeat after another may soon be transferred to measured space in audiation. That is, with sufficient capability, audiation of actual feeling of spatial distance between flicks in audiation renders prescribed physical movements unnecessary. Accurate placement of macrobeats is concomitant with consistent tempo, neither rushing nor slowing.

Chanting Rhythm Patterns

11. Chant a series of usual duple meter rhythm patterns based on four underlying macrobeats using neutral syllables (such as *bah*, *dah*, *mah*). Macro/microbeat and divisions patterns are best in the beginning. Do not use beat-function rhythm syllables yet. On the fourth macrobeat, students take a deep breath (to facilitate audiation) and repeat your pattern. That is, there is no pause between the end of your chanting and the beginning of students' chanting. Without a pause and maintaining consistent tempo, chant another rhythm pattern and students repeat it following the same procedure. Take full advantage of the fact most adolescents will quickly and enjoyably associate chanting with scat or rap performance. Negative attitudes about music, particularly singing, may possibly abate.

12. Students might physically indicate placement of macrobeats and microbeats as they chant, perhaps by moving heels up and down to macrobeats and arms back and forth together to microbeats, or if more-able students prefer, they may audiate macrobeats and microbeats. Either way, care is taken to maintain consistent tempo. Take time to be certain students are cognizant of placement of macrobeats and microbeats while chanting. If you determine students are chanting without concern for placement of macrobeats and microbeats, it may be because of lack of attention or coordination. When coordination is a problem, a review of the eleven coordination steps already described may be necessary.

13. Now beat-function rhythm syllables are used with the same rhythm patterns students chanted using neutral syllables.

14. Repeat suggestions 11, 12, and 13 above chanting usual triple meter rhythm patterns.

15. As students gain confidence and skill in chanting macro/microbeat and division patterns, introduce division/elongation, elongation, rest, tie, and upbeat patterns, first using neutral syllables and then beat-function rhythm syllables. Tie patterns are judiciously presented last.

Reading Rhythm Patterns

16. As learning sequence activities are being used, particularly with regard to music notation, be prepared for some students to volunteer note-value names and definitions of measure signatures they will describe as time or meter signatures. Whether they are sincerely trying to help you or seeking recognition is of no matter. What is important is you praise them and acknowledge you understand they have acquired information from their performance teachers and/or in music theory classes. They must remember what they have been taught because sometime in the future you will need their help and cooperation when making reference to that knowledge.

However, for the present time, you wish they would use their minds wisely by making comparisons and associations between what they have learned and what they are learning. You and they will enjoy great surprises pretending the class is starting with a blank slate.

17. Select and perform from notation students see a familiar or unfamiliar short melody in usual duple or triple meter of the difficulty level they have been taught to follow using note names. Notation with an abundance of beams rather than flags is preferable. Establish meter and tempo for students before they read and chant notation using beat-function rhythm syllables. Do not make reference to note values or measure signatures. Emphasize importance of audiating and associating beat-function rhythm syllables with durations when reading and not habitually reciting or thinking note-value names. Underscore feeling and audiating macrobeat and microbeat placement in the melody, not measure signatures, determines meter. You and students together arbitrarily identify rhythm patterns of two or four underlying macrobeats in length. Beams in notation are usually good guides for making selections.

18. You and students together read by chanting each rhythm pattern one at a time using beat-function rhythm syllables. Though inflections in artistic expression is expected, all durations in patterns are chanted on the same pitch so as not to suggest keyality or tonality. Separate rhythm patterns and take a deep breath before each is performed. Soon after students understand the logic of how beat-function rhythm syllables are associated with notation on the staff, guide them in identifying by themselves additional rhythm patterns. Exemplifying subjectivity in the identification of rhythm patterns, students take turns selecting rhythm patterns to read in ensemble using beat-function rhythm syllables.

19. Now the class reads all rhythm patterns in the melody continuously from beginning to end using beat-function rhythm syllables. Deep breaths are taken appropriately. There are no pauses between chanting of patterns. To do otherwise would distort tempo.

Rhythm Improvisation

20. After establishing a comfortable tempo, ask students to move to eight macrobeats and their division into two or three microbeats, depending upon the meter under consideration. Then ask them to audiate eight macrobeats in consistent tempo without prescribed movement. Now ask them to audiate a series of rhythm patterns superimposed on the eight underlying macrobeats. Given time to audiate, students take turns chanting individual improvisations.

21. Emphasize in improvisation there are no mistakes, only improper solutions. Nonetheless, students who continue to be dubious may be assisted by the class unobtrusively chanting macrobeats and microbeats or only macrobeats using neutral syllables as improvisations are being performed. To avert possible embarrassment, be prepared to conclude in a positive manner a student's uncompleted improvisation.

Rhythm Composition

22. After distributing blank staff paper, ask students to insert 2/4 or 6/8 or any another usual duple or triple measure signature. Direct them to mark off eight blank measures using bar lines, allowing sufficient space in each measure to accommodate whatever they may choose to compose. You may indicate on your own sheet of staff paper or at the board how all this is notated.

23. Audiating neutral or beat-function rhythm syllables for whatever rhythm pattern they choose, ask students to create in audiation a chant covering the eight measures and then, as they please, to notate it one measure at a time or all measures continuously.

Volunteers may perform their chants for the class as others listen critically and offer comments.

Whenever the opportunity presents itself, diplomatically call students' attention to the knowledge and skills they have acquired through learning sequence activities and use of rhythm syllables. Ask them if they ever thought it possible they could interpret rhythm notation without the imposition of counting, and how learning to improvise and compose rhythmically has increased their musical performance, enjoyment, and overall musical awareness. Patently explain if they apply the same effort to tonal development, their music achievement will increase exponentially when they are able to combine rhythm and tonal patterns into melodic patterns.

Tonal Development

1. While reviewing suggestion 2 under Rhythm Development in Part 4, keep in mind not only does free-flowing continuous movement refine consistency of tempo and meter when chanting rhythm patterns, it also promotes good intonation and expression when singing tonal patterns. Research suggests a contributing factor to this phenomenon is deep breathing coordinated with appropriate movement, which in turn engenders audiation before and during singing. I emphasize now and will remind you later of importance of taking the necessary time to persist in encouraging students to move and breath deeply as they are singing tonal patterns.

   A short review of tonalities, keyalities, and key signatures before moving on may be necessary. If deemed not, please skip to suggestion 2.

Tonalities and Keyalities

Tonality is not used in its ordinary sense. In common-practice music theory, tonality is defined either as the name given to a key signature (for example, E♭ given to the key signature of three flats) or as a combination-name given to a key signature and a mode (for example, E♭ major). For purposes of accuracy and clarity, tonality refers to what is usually called a mode, never simply a key signature. However, a mode does not only pertain to what is traditionally called modal music, such as Dorian or Mixolydian. Tonality is used because many persons assume if music is said to be in a mode it must be modal. They forget major and minor are also modes. There are at least eight tonalities: major, harmonic minor, Dorian, Phrygian, Lydian, Mixolydian, Aeolian, and Locrian.

It is necessary to consider and treat tonality and keyality apart from each other, as well as apart from a key signature. A key signature is a symbol. It is seen in notation. A keyality is a sign. It is heard in audiation. Various tonalities and keyalities may be associated with a key signature so, for example, the key signature of one sharp may indicate major tonality and G keyality, harmonic minor tonality and E keyality, Dorian tonality and A keyality, Mixolydian tonality and D keyality, and so on. Therefore, it is not possible to know keyality of music simply by seeing a key signature. Music needs to be audiated before its key signature may assume a keyality and tonality in audiation. The fifteen commonly named keyalities are C, G, D, A, E, B, F♯, C♯, F, B♭, E♭, A♭, D♭, G♭, and C♭. In music where tonality is major and keyality is C, one audiates *do* as resting tone and C as tonic. When audiating tonality, one audiates relations among several pitches, all of which in combination suggest a resting tone. However, when audiating keyality, audiation of only one pitch, the tonic, is necessary. For a more comprehensive discussion of tonality and related concepts, see my book, *Learning Sequences in Music: A Contemporary Music Learning Theory*. The book is listed in the Bibliography. For immediate concise definitions of terms, refer to the Glossary.

Tonal Syllables

To maximize audiation of tonality, the movable-*do* system with a *la* based minor offers most advantages of all tonal systems. Not only is *do* movable to correspond to keyality, syllable names change to correspond to the resting tone of a tonality. This change is indispensable to the development of audiation, which in turn affects reading and writing skills. Regardless of keyality, with *do* audiated as the resting tone, tonality is major; with *la*, harmonic minor or Aeolian; with *re*, Dorian; with *mi*, Phrygian; with *fa*, Lydian; with *so*, Mixolydian; and with *ti*, Locrian. In major tonality, any arrangement of *do mi so* is a tonic pattern; *so ti re fa*, a dominant-seventh pattern; and *fa la do* a subdominant pattern. In harmonic minor tonality, any arrangement of *la do mi* is a tonic pattern; *mi si ti re*, a dominant-seventh pattern; and *re fa la* a subdominant pattern. More information about tonal syllables may be found in Part 3, *Learning Sequence Activities for Middle and High School Students*, under Advanced Improvisation.

There are other advantages to the movable-*do* system with a *la* based minor. 1) Provision is made for chromatics with logically related but independent syllables, which allows for the verbal association of *si* in the fundamental tonality of harmonic minor as well as chromatic patterns in all tonalities. Ascending chromatic syllables are *di ri fi si li* and enharmonic descending chromatic syllables are *te le se me ra*. 2) Typical modulations in multitonal and multikeyal music (more broadly called atonal) can be performed without technical difficulties. 3) There are no consonant syllable endings. 4) Verbal associations remain logically consistent within a tonality regardless of keyality. For example, although syllables in the pattern *do mi so* have the same sound relation regardless of tonality or keyality in which they are found, they also have the benefit of relating to specific content, such as tonic in the context of major tonality and dominant in the context of Lydian tonality. Thus, audiation of tonal patterns is consistent within tonality, regardless of keyality.

Singing Tonal Patterns

2. Introduce tonal patterns by asking students to sing them in unison. A suitable tessitura for unchanged voices is from D above middle C to A or B♭, a fifth or minor sixth above, and the

prevailing range is from D above middle C to E, a tenth above. Boys with changing and changed voices may sing one octave below. The recommended range and tessitura take into consideration middle C is the approximate break between the speaking and singing voices. Of course, it is your decision to use keyalities and tessituras most suitable for your students.

3. Solo singing is not recommended initially, though in time it may be desirable with some individuals. It is of extreme importance tonality and keyality be firmly established before students begin to sing. That may be accomplished by you with or without students singing a short song in the tonality and keyality tonal patterns are to be sung, or more simply, tonic and dominant-seventh tonal patterns may be performed. Your singing of the first tonal pattern should establish a comfortable tempo for performing them all.

4. In major tonality, sing a series of tonal patterns using the neutral syllable *bum*, pausing and taking a deep breath before performing each one and making short pauses between each tonal pattern. Ask students to repeat what you have sung by singing in unison each tonal pattern one at a time. Begin with combinations of tonic and dominant-seventh patterns, emphasizing the leading tone in the dominant-seventh pattern moving to the tonic in the tonic pattern. It is important for purposes of intonation and expression students move upper parts of their body in a continuous free-flowing manner when they sing tonal patterns. Periodically remind students to audiate the tonic while they are singing other pitches, including those comprising the dominant-seventh pattern. Best intonation occurs when the pitch being sung is heard in conjunction (vertically) with the tonic and not in comparison to the previous or forthcoming pitch (horizontally).

5. For students who remain uncomfortable using their singing voice quality, rather than singing all pitches in a pattern, perhaps repetition of the tonic pitch for tonic patterns and the dominant pitch for dominant-seventh patterns might be

sufficient. A last option could be not to sing but to improvise movements as the class sings tonal patterns.

6. In time, follow the above procedure using tonal patterns in harmonic minor tonality. The keyality of D in harmonic minor tonality is recommended.

7. Now, using movable-do syllables, sing the same familiar tonal patterns that were performed using *bum* in suggestion 4.

8. When you determine students are familiar with tonic and dominant-seventh patterns in major and harmonic minor tonalities, using *bum* sing subdominant patterns combined in series with tonic and dominant-seventh patterns. However, emphasis is on tonic and dominant-seventh patterns. Subdominant patterns in major tonality are introduced first. It has been found in research subdominant patterns in harmonic minor tonality are difficult to audiate and perform, particularly those including the descending major sixth interval.

9. Now, using movable-do syllables, sing the same familiar tonal patterns that were performed using *bum*.

10. There are more functions than tonic, dominant-seventh, and subdominant patterns in the various tonalities. As you wish and deem it prudent, these functions may be taught to students. Although major and harmonic minor tonalities share the same pattern functions, not all, but additional ones, are found in other tonalities. The pattern functions in other tonalities are presented below in notational form.

HARMONIC MINOR

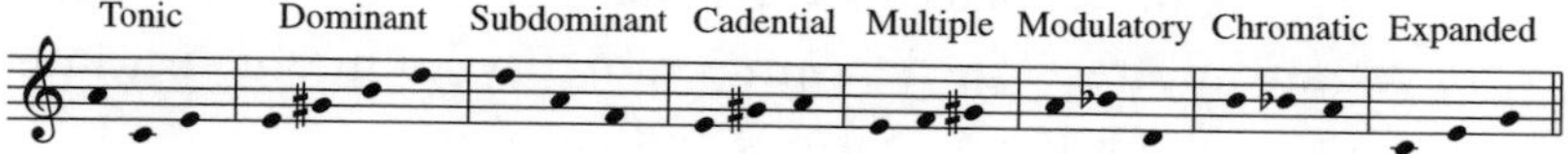

Reading Tonal Patterns

11. As with rhythm reading, be prepared for some students to volunteer note letter-names and definitions of key signatures used by music theorists. As you deal with their comments in a way similar to interaction concerning their offering note-value names and definitions of measure signatures, explain why you use *do* signature in place of key signature. If you believe students have an interest in learning more, you might initiate a discussion about key signatures and keyality.

12. Select and perform from notation a familiar or unfamiliar short melody of the difficulty level students are able to follow or read using note letter-names. Using movable-*do* syllables, establish tonality and keyality for students before they begin to read notation vocally and instrumentally.

13. Remind students of where *do* is placed on the staff with either or both the treble and bass clef. Sing *do* with students and explain if *do* is on a line, *mi* and *so* will be on the next two lines above and *ti* on the space below *do*. Similarly, if *do* is on a space, *mi* and *so* will be on the next two spaces above and *ti* is on the line below *do*. Assist students, as necessary, in logically associating syllables with other lines and spaces.

14. You and students together arbitrarily identify tonal patterns of from two to four, the majority being three, notes in length. Rhythm patterns are usually good guides for making selections, but choices need not coincide with rhythm patterns for purposes of reading.

15. You and students together read by singing each tonal pattern that has been identified one at a time using movable-*do* syllables. Separate tonal patterns and take a deep breath before each is performed. Be certain all pitches are of equal duration so as not to convey rhythm or meter.

16. Soon after students understand the logic of the placement of syllables on the staff, guide them in identifying by themselves remaining tonal patterns. Individual students take turns in selecting tonal patterns for the class to read in ensemble.

17. Now the class reads all tonal patterns in the melody one at a time from beginning to end using movable-*do* syllables. Pauses and deep breaths are still observed.

Tonal Improvisation

18. Ask students to audiate eight macrobeats in usual duple meter. Then you and students individually and/or in ensemble perform

a series of rhythm patterns superimposed on eight underlying macrobeats using one or more neutral syllables. Macro/microbeat and division patterns are best, but other functions may also be used. Ask students individually to perform a series of rhythm patterns extending over eight underlying macrobeats using neutral or beat-function rhythm syllables.

19. Establish major tonality and usual duple meter. Then, each student using the series of rhythm patterns they performed, or they may concurrently improvise rhythm patterns, sing pitches in the tonic pattern for the first-four underlying macrobeats, pitches in the dominant-seventh pattern for the next two underlying macrobeats, and for the final two underlying macrobeats again sing pitches in the tonic pattern. Only pitches in the specific patterns may be used. That is, any arrangement of only *do mi so* may be used with tonic patterns and only *so ti re fa* with dominant-seventh patterns.

20. Follow the same procedure but replace the dominant-seventh chord with the subdominant chord. Pitches in the tonic chord are sung for the first-four underlying macrobeats, pitches in the subdominant chord are sung for the next two underlying macrobeats, and pitches in the tonic chord are sung again for the last two macrobeats. Only *fa la do* may be used with subdominant patterns.

21. Follow the same procedure but now all three chords are included in the improvisation. Pitches in the tonic chord are sung for the first-two underlying macrobeats, pitches in the subdominant chord are sung for the next two underlying macrobeats, pitches in the dominant-seventh chord are sung for the next two underlying macrobeats, and the tonic chord is sung again for the last two underlying macrobeats.

22. Follow the same procedure for major tonality and usual triple meter, harmonic minor tonality and usual duple meter, and harmonic minor tonality and usual triple meter. Remember,

before students are asked to perform any type of improvisation, meter and tonality must be firmly established.

Tonal Composition

23. After distributing blank staff paper, ask students to insert the measure signature 4/4 and the *do* signature of two sharps. You may care to substitute another usual duple measure signature and/or *do* signature to be used with major tonality. Direct students to mark off eight blank measures using bar lines, allowing sufficient space in each measure to accommodate whatever they may choose to compose. You may indicate on your own sheet of staff paper or at the board how all is notated.
24. Show students how to indicate Roman numerals above each of the eight measures to indicate chord functions: I for tonic, V7 for dominant-seventh, and IV for subdominant.
25. Establish D keyality in major tonality and usual duple meter.
26. Audiating whatever rhythm patterns they choose, ask students to create in audiation a melody covering eight measures and then, as they please, to notate it one measure at a time or all at once. They may use one or more chord functions in a measure, and a sequence may be repeated in contiguous measures.
27. Volunteers may sing their melodies for the class. Other students listen critically and offer comments.
28. Follow the same procedure for creating compositions in harmonic minor tonality, using only I, V7, and IV and in usual triple meter.
29. The pinnacle of this activity might be to encourage students to notate their compositions for various instrumental ensembles.

Reading Melodic Patterns

30. After you establish meter and tempo, students look at the notation of a familiar or unfamiliar short melody. Ask them to

scan the melody and subjectively identify and audiate rhythm patterns in the melody by using beat-function rhythm syllables. That is, they only audiate, not perform, rhythm patterns. Then establish tonality and keyality, and beginning pitch if necessary, and ask them to scan the melody and subjectively identify and audiate tonal patterns in the melody by using movable-*do* syllables. Again, they only audiate, not perform, tonal patterns. Now ask them to notationally audiate (read silently not singing or chanting) the melody, observing both tonal and rhythm components simultaneously.

31. Giving students a few minutes to audiate the melody, ask them to read and perform vocally the melody in entirety using one or more neutral syllables or the text of the song. Neither tonal syllables nor rhythm syllables are to be performed when reading melodic patterns, only audiated in unique ways students find comfortable.

Harmonic Improvisation and Melodic Patterns

32. Being knowledgeable about tonal syllables and rhythm syllables, students discover the transition from notational audiation to audiation for purposes of harmonic improvisation is accomplished with ease. Rather than performing syllabic tonal patterns as arpeggios, now the all pitches in the arpeggio are performed as a chord. Notated on the following page are two harmonic progressions, each comprising three chords in major tonality. The first includes tonic, dominant-seventh, tonic. The second includes tonic, subdominant, tonic. Underneath are two harmonic progressions, each similarly comprising three chords in harmonic minor tonality. Roman numerals and tonal syllables are indicated under each chord in the harmonic progressions.

Major Tonality

Harmonic Minor Tonality

33. Ask students to audiate eight macrobeats in usual duple meter. Then you and students individually and/or in ensemble perform a series of rhythm patterns superimposed on eight underlying macrobeats using one or more neutral syllables. Macro/microbeat and division patterns are best, but all other functions may be used.

34. Divide the class into three sections. Each section sings one of the pitches in the tonic chord in major tonality using tonal syllables. Adhering to the voice leadings in the notated harmonic progressions, follow the same procedure for the dominant-seventh chord. With that satisfactorily accomplished, students quietly sing the tonic, dominant-seventh, tonic progression humming or using one or more neutral syllables. The progression is based on eight underlying macrobeats. As notated below, the tonic chord is sung for the first-four underlying macrobeats, the dominant-seventh chord for the next two underlying macrobeats, and the tonic chord for the last two underlying macrobeats.

35. As the class sings repetitions of the harmonic progression, students take turns improvising a melody over the harmonic progression. Only the three pitches constituting the chord being sung but any rhythm patterns may be used in the improvisation. Non-harmonic tones are not included at this time. Until students develop self-confidence in improvising solo, several students may initially improvise at the same time.

37. Follow the same procedure outlined in steps 33, 34, and 35 above replacing the dominant-seventh chord with the subdominant chord. As notated below, the tonic chord is sung for the first-four underlying macrobeats, the subdominant chord for the next two underlying macrobeats, and the tonic chord for the last two underlying macrobeats.

38. Following the same procedure outlined in steps 33, 34, and 35 above, now all three chords are included in the harmonic progression. As notated below, the tonic chord is sung for the first-two underlying macrobeats, the subdominant chord for the next two underlying macrobeats, the dominant-seventh chord for the next two underlying macrobeats, and the tonic chord for the last two underlying macrobeats.

39. If individual students find improvising a melody over harmonic progressions initially overwhelming, they may begin by singing only roots of chords, constituting a root melody. The entire class may sing root melodies before more complex melodies. Whenever you believe only pitches in each triad are solidified in audiation, suggest students use non-harmonic pitches in their improvisations. After students are comfortable improvising melodies in major tonality and usual duple meter, suggestions 33

through 35 may be followed to guide students in improvising in major tonality and usual triple meter, harmonic minor tonality and usual duple meter, and harmonic minor tonality and usual triple meter. For more details, read Improvisation in Part 3, Learning Sequence Activities for Middle and High School Instrumental Students.

Creative Composition and Melodic Patterns

40. Procedures for composing using melodic patterns based on harmonic progressions have much in common with composing using tonal patterns. After distributing blank staff paper, ask students to insert the measure signature 4/4 and the *do* signature of two sharps. Direct them to mark off eight blank measures using bar lines, allowing sufficient space in each measure to accommodate whatever they may choose to compose. You may indicate on your own sheet of staff paper or at the board how all is notated.

41. Show students how to indicate one chord symbol or Roman numerals above each of the eight measures. For example, the harmonic progression might be D, G, A7, D, G, D, A7, D or I, IV, V7, I, IV, I, V7, I.

42. Establish D keyality in major tonality and usual duple meter.

43. Audiating whatever rhythm patterns they choose, ask students to create in audiation a melody covering eight measures and then, as they please, to notate it one measure at a time or all at once. Chord pitches and non-harmonic tones may be used in accordance with the harmonic progression.

44. Volunteers may sing their melodies for the class as the other students sing the harmonic progression. They also listen critically and offer comments.

45. Follow the same procedure for creating compositions in harmonic minor tonality and usual triple meter.

46. The pinnacle of this activity might be to encourage students to notate arrangements of their compositions for various instrumental ensembles. With their developed skills in audiating tonal syllables and notational audiation, transpositions should be well understood and easy to accomplish.

47. If students are not already astonished by realizing for themselves they now can truly read music notation and there is no longer a need for them to perfunctorily decode symbols, alert them to the fact audiation is primarily responsible for improving their musicianship. True, a scant few may have already been able to hear the sound of music notation without consulting a music instrument, but in all probability even they were achieving that in a boring and mechanical rather than an artistic manner. Underscore notational audiation is one advantage of having learned to use tonal syllables and rhythm syllables. Other benefits are their abilities to improvise and create music.

48. Suggestion 5 under Different Methods and Teachers in Part 2, Transitioning Learning Sequence Activities to Traditional Activities for Elementary School Instrumental Students Graduating to Upper Grades, includes a model packet of terminology and definitions pertaining to music theory. Before students leave your tutelage and work with other teachers and study with students who use traditional terminology, it might be well for them to become familiar with customary terminology. Thus, the packet, or one you have compiled, may be reproduced and a copy given to each student. After explaining its content, suggest to students they might keep the material for further reference as necessary.

Part 5

Including New Students in Learning Sequence Activities, Using Learning Sequence Activities in Combined-Grades Classroom Music, and Record Keeping

Consequences of absence of and discontinuity in music curriculums in elementary and secondary schools were discussed in the Introduction. The effect on students in a fixed group notwithstanding, the situation becomes profound when students transfer from one school to another in the same school district, but especially egregious when students move from one city to another. Thus, classroom music teachers and music specialists can entertain virtually no expectation of what knowledge and musical skills a new student might possess. Because familiarity with music learning theory and learning sequence activities is not widespread, a teacher who instructs according to these concepts encounters unusual obstacles when integrating new students into ongoing classroom procedures and ensemble rehearsals. That is not to minimize disadvantages to students. Somehow this chasm between learning sequence activities and common place instruction must be bridged if music education is to have lasting and worthwhile value for students as yet unexposed to research-based pedagogy. How this might be accomplished is explained herein in Part 5.

If instruction is being based on music learning theory, you are aware skill learning sequence comprises levels and sublevels, as do tonal learning sequence and rhythm learning sequence. Moreover, you are familiar with each level and sublevel of the three components. How these levels and sublevels interact within each theory and how skill, tonal, and rhythm learning theories interact with one another provide the foundation for practical applications of learning sequence activities. However, it may be helpful to review my book, *Learning Sequences in Music: A Contemporary Music Learning Theory*. It is listed in the Bibliography. Also, brief summaries of music learning theory and learning sequence activities are presented in Part 6.

Integrating New Students

Results of a music aptitude test will provide you with valuable information for familiarizing yourself with the musical potential of students new to your classroom. For elementary and middle school students, the *Primary Measures of Music Audiation*, or the *Intermediate Measures of Music Audiation* is recommended for administration. For high school students, the *Advanced Measures of Music Audiation* and *Musical Aptitude Profile* are appropriate. Information pertaining to these and other tests may be found in *Introduction to Research and the Psychology of Music* and *Music Aptitude and Related Tests* (G-5719), a brochure published by GIA and offered free of charge. Both are mine and are listed in the Bibliography. Test results will guide you in teaching to individual musical differences among new students and how those overall differences compare with collective potential of students with whom you are already familiar. When students' individual musical needs are taken into account, those with limited potential will not become frustrated and those with exceptional potential will not become bored. Preliminary time spent reading test manuals and ancillary books about the interpretation and use of music aptitude test results will be rewarding.

As elucidated in Part 1, Movement and Interactive Breathing as Readiness for Learning Rhythm, it is important students are guided in affiliating their body with free-flowing continuous movement in physical space to learn as much as their music potential will allow. This activity will assist them in making a smooth and confident transition to singing tonal patterns as well as chanting rhythm patterns in learning sequence activities. Performing tonal and rhythm patterns provides foundation for satisfactory participation in learning sequence activities at all levels and sublevels of music learning theory.

Time may not allow you to shepherd students in their movements corresponding to pedagogical suggestions for all twenty-four melodies in Part 1. If only a few can be covered, it will be sufficient to attend to only the first-four melodies in which just upper parts of the body are used. Whatever the circumstances, you will find it advantageous to scan the entire set of melodies and suggestions before any instruction in movement is initiated.

Students who are engaging in learning sequence activities are, of course, receiving instruction from you at a specific level or sublevel of skill learning sequence and specific levels or sublevels of tonal learning sequence or rhythm learning sequence. At the beginning or during the year, new students with no understanding of learning sequence activities may enter your class. What do you do? Although the following solutions are not ideal because it is not possible to remediate students' deficits, it is possible to offer them compensatory instruction. This means, depending on many factors including their musical limitations, students probably will not achieve to the extent their musical potential would have allowed if they had begun receiving instruction in learning sequence activities at an earlier age.

Assume you are currently teaching Tonal Unit 2 in *Tonal Register Book One*. The skill (in terms of skill learning sequence) is Verbal Association and the content (in terms of tonal learning sequence) is Tonic and Dominant/Major and Minor. Your objective during the ten minutes of learning sequence activities is to have students successfully sing solo either individual easy, moderately difficult, or difficult tonal patterns as directed by their music aptitude test results. It is by singing tonal patterns solo at the aural/oral and verbal association levels of skill learning sequence students acquire a personal vocabulary of tonal patterns that will necessarily serve them as instruction advances to remaining levels of discrimination learning and all levels of inference learning.

Consider the following example. You have established context by singing the tonal sequence (*so la so fa mi re ti do*) in major tonality. Then students repeat tonal patterns you have sung using movable-*do* syllables. After singing class patterns, students begin to sing individual tonal patterns. *All students sing class tonal patterns but only students who are not new to the class are asked to sing individual tonal patterns solo. New students do not sing individual tonal patterns solo until the next aural/oral unit (Tonal Unit 4) is introduced through bridging movement.* In Unit 4, the same tonalities (content level) are repeated at the aural/oral level and therefore, new students will have sufficient opportunity to audiate and become familiar with major and harmonic minor tonalities before they are expected to sing tonal patterns solo in major and harmonic minor tonalities using *bum* and later using movable-*do* tonal syllables at the verbal association level of learning.

Bridging movement occurred from Tonal Unit 2 to Tonal Unit 3 and back to Tonal Unit 4. Creativity/Improvisation-verbal at Tonal Unit 3 was the intermediate level of skill learning between two Aural/Oral Units. There are eight aural/oral levels scattered among the forty-two units incorporating learning sequence activities in *Tonal Register Books One* and *Two*.

Objectives have logical order when they progress by step sequentially from achievement at one level or sublevel of learning to the next higher level or sublevel of learning, or when they progress by skip to make a bridge from one level or sublevel of learning to achievement at any higher level or sublevel of learning. The first type of progression is called forward stepwise movement and the second forward bridging movement. Stepwise and bridging movement may also be used to take students back to lower levels and sublevels of learning for purposes of review, to make up what was previously purposefully or inadvertently skipped over, and most importantly, to introduce them to additional patterns in a familiar tonality or to a new level of skill or tonal or rhythm learning sequence. However, although achievement at a given level may be temporarily postponed, it may never be indefinitely neglected.

Assign students who are familiar with learning sequence activities to be companions to new students. The experienced student of each pair quietly explains to the new student what you are teaching, why you are teaching it, and how students are expected to respond. Also, when you call upon the new student to repeat at the next aural/oral level an individual tonal pattern solo, initially the partner, using discretion, may join the new student in duet during the teaching mode to instill his or her confidence in the procedure. Similar efforts may be made to avoid the new student's possible embarrassment or failure. If necessary, the duet may carry forth when the new student is asked to sing in the evaluation mode until both you and your assistant believe the new student is capable of truly singing solo. At the end of the week, or at another time you deem appropriate, the student who is assisting gives you a verbal report on how the new student is acclimating. This information is important for offering appropriate future instruction, particularly to the new student.

Follow the same procedure explained in suggestions above when rhythm learning sequence is combined with skill learning sequence. For example, assume you are currently teaching Rhythm Unit 1 in *Rhythm Register Book One*. The skill (in terms of skill learning sequence) is Aural/Oral and the content (in terms of rhythm learning sequence) is Macro/Microbeats/Usual Duple and Triple. Your objective during the ten minutes of learning sequence activities is to have students successfully chant solo either individual easy, moderately difficult, or difficult rhythm patterns as directed by their music aptitude test results.

You have established context by chanting the rhythm sequence (*du be du* | *du be du*) in usual duple meter. Then students repeat rhythm patterns you have chanted using beat function rhythm syllables. After chanting class patterns, students begin to chant rhythm patterns. *All students chant class rhythm patterns but only students who are <u>not</u> new to the class are asked to chant individual rhythm patterns solo. New students* *do not chant individual rhythm patterns solo until the next aural/oral unit (Rhythm Unit 3) is introduced through stepwise movement.* In Unit 3, the same meters (content level) are repeated at the aural/oral level and therefore, new students will have sufficient opportunity to audiate and become familiar with usual duple and triple meters before they are expected to chant rhythm patterns solo in usual duple and triple meters using *bah* and later using beat function rhythm syllables at the verbal association of learning. As with tonal learning sequence, assign experienced students to assist new students when rhythm patterns are being performed.

Stepwise movement occurred from Rhythm Unit 1 to Unit 2 and back to Unit 3. Verbal Association at Tonal Unit 2 was the intermediate level of skill learning between two Aural/Oral Units. There are eight aural/oral levels scattered among the forty-two units incorporating skill learning sequence in *Rhythm Register Books One* and *Two*. Thus, there is ample opportunity for new students to become comfortable audiating usual duple and triple meters before they are expected to chant rhythm patterns solo in usual duple and triple meters using *bah* and later using beat function rhythm syllables at the verbal association level of learning. As a result, they will be advantageously integrated into regular classroom procedures.

Combined-Grades Classroom Music

Occasionally when finances become limited, school administrators combine two or more small classes of students into one classroom requiring only one teacher. Critics are not pleased with this economy measure because they believe it puts an undue burden on the teacher, and that may be true. However, there are other persons who are of the opinion one-room school houses, common place in the early history of the country, should have never been discontinued and replaced with consolidated schools comprising individual grade classrooms. After all, some of the greatest minds emerged from groups of students who varied in age from five to twelve years and were taught together as an intact group. Obviously, as alert younger students were studying, they listened to what older students were being taught. When it later became their turn to learn what they overheard taught to older students, they excelled because of readiness provided indirectly. And, of course, older students were assigned to assist younger students in their studies, and all students were expected to fulfill consigned duties. In addition to academic pursuits, students developed a sense of responsibility and an understanding of the need to contribute to the education of their younger counterparts.

When students in different grades are grouped in a single classroom, it is possible to teach them music successfully according to principles of music learning theory and learning sequence activities. Some groups will be taught lower numbered units and other groups higher numbered units. Though the situation may not be ideal, it does, as explained, offer advantages. Disadvantages are that you, the teacher, must engage in additional preparation, accomplish more than is normally expected by teaching with alacrity because of less time available to guide each group and individual students, and maintain divergent records of students' achievement. Conditions that may seem undesirable notwithstanding, it is beneficial for students to receive some instruction in learning sequence activities than none at all. Assuming your familiarity with learning sequence activities, only sparse recommendations for facilitating instruction under the described novel conditions are necessary.

— Prepare a set of *Tonal Register Books One* and *Two* and *Rhythm Register Books One* and *Two* for separate groups of students being taught.

— Teach different groups of students learning sequence activities at various times of the day, spread apart as much as possible. Sessions at the beginning, middle, and end of the day are preferable. Much of what is necessary can be accomplished in ten minute sessions but if time is a factor, each session may be only five minutes.

— Teach either a Tonal Unit or a Rhythm Unit to all groups during a given day. The same skill and/or tonal or rhythm content need not be taught to all groups. In fact, diversity is recommended.

— Teach one or more Tonal Units and Rhythm Units on alternate weeks.

Record Keeping

As explained in the *Reference Handbook for Using Learning Sequence Activities*, there is a Seating/Evaluation Chart on each page of *Tonal Register Books One* and *Two and Rhythm Register Books One* and *Two*. Every chart includes forty-eight boxes. According to where they are seated in the classroom, individual student names and music aptitude test results are written in each box. Students who score high (80th percentile and above) have a line placed above their name, students who score low (20th percentile and below) have a line placed below their names, and no line is drawn for students whose score is average (from the 21st to 79th percentile). Information on the chart need not be rewritten on each page of the register books if a master chart is organized at the beginning of instruction and multiple duplicates are made on a copy machine. Then, duplicates are pasted over each blank seating chart. Of course, individual student's music aptitude test results will be different on Seating/Evaluation charts in the *Tonal Register Books* and *Rhythm Register Books*.

An immediate record is made on the Seating/Evaluation Chart of each student's performance of solo patterns in the teaching and evaluation modes. In the teaching mode, you sing or chant in duet with the student when asked to perform a pattern solo. In that way the student builds trust in you to prevent possible embarrassment if he or she cannot or does not perform the pattern successfully. As you and the student sing, you listen carefully to determine if the student is reasonably capable of singing or chanting the pattern. If so, the next time the student is asked to sing or chant the solo pattern you give a familiar gesture indicating you will perform in duet again as you did before in the teaching mode. However, this time you remain silent as the student performs in the evaluation mode. If you decide after either the teaching mode or evaluation mode the student still requires your assistance, you continue performing with the student in the teaching mode until you are given evidence the student is ready to perform solo successfully in the evaluation mode.

When a student performs the easy pattern acceptably in the teaching mode, a single vertical line is made in the appropriate box on the Seating/Evaluation Chart. By marking the box that way you will know the next time you gesture to the student he or she is to perform the easy pattern solo in the evaluation mode. When the student successfully performs the pattern in the evaluation mode, the single line is crossed. By looking at the Seating/Evaluation Chart it can be quickly discerned the next time you gesture to the student to perform a pattern, it will be the moderately difficult pattern in the teaching mode. Next the student will perform the moderately difficult pattern in the evaluation mode. At that time there will be two crossed lines in the student's box. The process is repeated for the difficult pattern and then there will be three crossed lines in the box.

Depending upon a student's musical potential as indicated by music aptitude test results, there may be no lines or from one vertical line to three crossed lines in each box. Keeping such records provides for thoughtful and precise instruction during the school year that is not wasteful of time and energy and takes into account students' individual musical needs in terms of their individual musical differences.

Record keeping of students' achievement becomes somewhat complex from year-to-year even if you are to teach all students in some ensuing years. That is so because rarely do students remain as an intact group when graduating from one grade to another. Thus, marked pages in the Register Books are removed and stapled together so easy reference can be made to them by you or another teacher when the new year begins. You may keep the sets of pages in your office or file them in a main school office. Through an examination of the average achievement of newly assembled groups of students, it is possible to make an informed decision concerning which Tonal Unit and Rhythm Unit would be best to initiate instruction in the new year. Of course, there will be units that serve as a review for some students whereas other units may be a little advanced for other students. Take that into consideration when asking students to perform in both the teaching and evaluation modes. Some students will require extra attention when performing in the teaching mode while it may be prudent to skip the teaching mode for others and move directly to the evaluation mode as a review. In the case of advanced students, new markings may be made in the blank boxes or those inserted the previous year may be recopied. If previous marking are used, which I recommend, students who have already been evaluated by performing solo patterns may perform only class patterns and direct their attention to assisting students who are unfamiliar with the Tonal or Rhythm Unit currently under consideration. However, it is not recommended different Units comprising different levels of skill and tonal or rhythm learning sequences be taught at the same time to different students in the same group in an attempt to accommodate individual musical needs. That would complicate learning and instruction.

Part 6

Introducing College and University Music Students to Learning Sequence Activities

Music learning theory provides rationale for using learning sequence activities when teaching college and university music students as well as elementary and secondary school students music. Thus, in the event you are not familiar with music learning theory and learning sequence activities or want to review, brief summaries are presented below. They need not be studied in great detail. All that is required when teaching your students is to follow the organization of the *Tonal Register Books* and *Rhythm Register Books* page by page. By doing so, you will knowingly present to your students levels of skill, tonal content, and rhythm content in their proper sequence. Also, tonal patterns and rhythm patterns to be taught sequentially are notated on each page of the *Register Books* according to their difficulty levels. For more comprehensive information with explanations about skill learning sequence, tonal learning sequence, rhythm learning sequence, and tonal pattern and rhythm pattern hierarchies, read my book, *Learning Sequences in Music: A Contemporary Music Learning Theory*. It is listed in the Bibliography.

Music Learning Theory

In terms of music learning theory, discrimination and inference are two generic types of learning. Discrimination learning is fundamental, because it provides necessary readiness for inference learning which is more conceptual. Imitation is crucial to discrimination learning, and it provides the basis for later generalization and abstraction in inference learning. However, discrimination and inference learning are not mutually exclusive. They occur together as one or the other receives greater emphasis.

Students engage in discrimination learning when they are conscious of being taught but do not fully understand what they are being taught or why they are being taught. For example, when students learn to perform through imitation, they are engaging in discrimination learning, because they are learning to discriminate among pitches, durations, tonal patterns, rhythm patterns, tonalities, and meters. Inference learning, on the other hand, occurs when students are unconscious of what they are learning or even that they are learning, because they are teaching themselves to learn what is unfamiliar by inferring from what is familiar.

The more facts and ideas students can discriminate among, the more inferences they are able to make. Though a teacher cannot teach students what to infer, a teacher can teach students not only how best to discriminate, but how best to teach themselves to make inferences. In other words, although a teacher can teach students both how and what to learn at the discrimination level, a teacher can only guide students in how to learn at the inference level.

As outlined below, there are five levels and two sublevels of discrimination learning, and three levels and three sublevels of inference learning. After each level or sublevel of discrimination learning is achieved, it is incorporated into and interacts with the next stepwise higher level or sublevel of discrimination learning. Similarly, after each level or sublevel of inference learning is achieved, it is incorporated into and interacts with the next higher stepwise level or sublevel of inference learning. Ultimately, discrimination learning is absorbed into inference learning.

Discrimination Learning

AURAL/ORAL

VERBAL ASSOCIATION

PARTIAL SYNTHESIS

SYMBOLIC ASSOCIATION
Reading and Writing

COMPOSITE SYNTHESIS
Reading and Writing

Inference Learning

GENERALIZATION
Aural/Oral, Verbal, and Symbolic
Reading and Writing

CREATIVITY/IMPROVISATION
Aural/Oral and Symbolic
Reading and Writing

THEORETICAL UNDERSTANDING
Aural/Oral, Verbal, and Symbolic
Reading and Writing

Discrimination Learning

Aural/Oral

The most elementary level of discrimination learning is aural/oral. It provides necessary readiness for every other level of discrimination learning as well as for all levels of inference learning. In aural/oral learning, hearing music involves the aural process and performing music the oral process. Moving rhythmically, with or without singing or chanting, is considered part of the oral process. At the aural/oral level, students learn to recognize a pattern, for example, simply by hearing it repeatedly. Thus, the aural part of aural/oral has been engaged without the oral part. Only when students imitate by singing or chanting using neutral syllables what they have heard does the oral part of aural/oral come to the fore. It is through the aural part of aural/oral learning students acquire a listening vocabulary of tonal patterns and rhythm patterns, and it is through the oral part of aural/oral learning students acquire a performing vocabulary of tonal patterns and rhythm patterns. With that accomplished, circular aural/oral feedback, which is necessary for audiation, becomes possible. In a word, without aural/oral achievement none of the other levels of discrimination learning and no level of inference learning will be achieved satisfactorily.

The extent to which students learn how to audiate depends not only on their music aptitude but on size of their aural and oral tonal pattern and rhythm pattern vocabularies. Just as the word is the basic unit of meaning in language, so the pattern is the basic unit of meaning in music. It is words, not individual letters, that make possible our understanding of language, and so the more words students have in their listening and speaking vocabularies, the better they are able to think about what is said to them and the better able they are to make and to draw conclusions of their own. In music, it is patterns, not individual pitches or durations, that make audiation possible. An individual pitch or duration has only possibilities for meaning, but because a pattern of pitches or durations does have meaning, the more tonal patterns and rhythm patterns students have in their listening and performance vocabularies, the better able they will be to audiate, that is, to conceptualize from and to form generalizations about music they are hearing or producing.

Verbal Association

At the aural/oral level, we give internal musical meaning to what we are audiating. At the verbal association level, in addition to carrying forth internal musical meaning, such as tonality and meter, we also give external meaning to what we are audiating. External meaning may relate, for example, to the association of note letter-names, time-value names, names of intervals, tonal syllables, and rhythm syllables Unless internal meaning is solidified, applying external meaning is difficult and confusing.

For example, consider a pattern appearing near the beginning and again near the end of a song. The pattern may have the same label, for example, E C, but it will be audiated differently, depending on patterns preceding and following it, because in each instance it is the context of complete series of patterns that is audiated. A similar situation occurs with notation. When the same notated pattern is surrounded by different patterns, it too will be audiated differently each time depending on context. It is imperative the aural/oral and verbal association levels of learning be taught separately. Contextual understanding at the aural/oral level must be developed before verbal association is introduced.

Students learn to respond through audiation to a broad range of music as a result of developing tonal pattern and rhythm pattern vocabularies. Without verbal association, students are increasingly at a disadvantage to discriminate among additional patterns they need to learn. As students learn more and more patterns using neutral syllables, patterns will begin to sound alike unless they are organized by syllable names in audiation. Verbal association makes possible students' retention and recall of patterns, tonalities, and meters for use in higher levels of discrimination learning and in all levels of inference learning. This is particularly true in creativity/improvisation, because without verbal association, even patterns that were once secure in audiation at the aural/oral level using neutral syllables may be lost.

Tonal syllables and rhythm syllables are learned not only to retain patterns in audiation, but to teach oneself additional patterns. Obviously, it is not possible to teach students all patterns they will ultimately need to know or want to know by relying on discrimination learning alone. Patterns taught using tonal syllables and rhythm syllables in discrimination learning are what provide students with readiness to teach themselves unfamiliar patterns in inference learning. Just as we think with words for the most part formed logically from roots, prefixes, and suffixes, so we audiate in music with verbal associations that have internal logic. In learning sequence activities, students become conscious of what they are audiating through the use of syllables. In traditional teaching, when sound and syllables are taught simultaneously, usually students become conscious of syllables apart from sound.

Partial Synthesis

In music learning theory, discrimination learning incorporates both partial synthesis and composite synthesis levels of learning. The aural/oral and verbal association levels of learning are assimilated (synthesized) into the partial synthesis level of learning, and the partial synthesis and symbolic association levels of learning are assimilated (synthesized) into the composite synthesis level of learning.

The partial synthesis level operates in two ways. First, as students assimilate aural/oral and verbal association levels, they become aware of internal logic of tonal syllables within and among tonal patterns and internal logic of rhythm syllables within and among rhythm patterns. Thus, at the partial synthesis level of discrimination learning, inference learning begins to take place in students' audiation. Second, at the partial synthesis level, students learn to synthesize individual patterns they are audiating into series of tonal patterns or rhythm patterns. When students hear a pattern as part of a series, they audiate and perform it differently, depending on the way it interacts with other patterns in the series, and thus they learn to audiate pattern relationships. To students' ears, the whole becomes different from, but not necessarily greater than, the sum of its parts.

Symbolic Association-reading and writing

At the next level of discrimination learning, symbolic association, students are taught to read and write, in both familiar and unfamiliar order, familiar tonal patterns and rhythm patterns in familiar tonalities and meters they learned to audiate and label at the aural/oral, verbal association, and partial synthesis levels of learning.

Symbolic association is not to be confused with what is commonly called music theory. Reading and writing music notation has as little relation to a theory of music as reading and writing a language has to linguistic theory. Music theory, in its true meaning, is an integral part of theoretical understanding, the highest level of inference learning. In music learning theory, note letter-names, time-value names, and definitions of key signatures and measure signatures and other symbols are taught and serve only as techniques for achieving some objectives associated with notation and the theoretical understanding level of learning.

When students are taught sequentially aural/oral, verbal association, and partial synthesis levels of learning before they read and write music notation, they are able to audiate what they see in notation without consulting an instrument. With emphasis on association at the symbolic association level, this is especially so because students not only learn to associate symbols in notation with names of tonalities and meters already familiar in audiation to them, but also with sounds of patterns and syllables associated with those sounds.

In symbolic association, students learn to read tonal patterns and rhythm patterns. That is, individual pitches and durations are not given consideration, just as in the Chinese language, for example, which has no alphabet, logographs are read and written as complete words, and individual characters are not given consideration. Unfortunately, when students are not taught how to audiate, they force an alphabet on music notation, focusing on individual note letter-names instead of series of pitches and individual time-value names instead of series of durations. Thus, they learn to decode notation because they cannot audiate. For students who can audiate, however, notation becomes a picture of what they are audiating.

Composite Synthesis-reading and writing

Composite synthesis, the highest level of discrimination learning, serves the same function in synthesizing partial synthesis and the symbolic association levels of learning as partial synthesis serves in synthesizing aural/oral and the verbal association levels of learning. At the composite synthesis level, students learn to audiate tonality or meter of one or more series of familiar tonal patterns or rhythm patterns in familiar or unfamiliar order as they are reading or writing patterns, using skills they learned both at the partial synthesis and symbolic association levels of learning. Specifically, students are now audiating tonality or meter at the same time they are reading or writing series of patterns, so although at the partial synthesis level musically intelligent listening is taking place, now, at the composite synthesis level, musically intelligent reading and writing in addition to musically intelligent listening are taking place. In symbolic association, students are simply reading and writing, whereas in composite synthesis, they are reading and writing contextually.

Of course, with continued use, skills, tonal patterns, and rhythm patterns students teach themselves at inference levels of learning will become familiar to them, and the number of patterns that become familiar to students will increase as you continue to expose them to additional unfamiliar tonal patterns and rhythm patterns. Students are engaged in inference learning even though in time they become familiar with a novel pattern or inference skill, because they are engaging in inference learning every time they teach themselves new and better ways to use the pattern or skill. Nonetheless, it simply is not possible for even an accomplished musician to ever become familiar with all conceivable patterns in music and to know how to generalize, create, improvise, and theorize about them to the fullest.

Inference Learning

Students are taught in discrimination learning to audiate, read, and write music with familiar patterns in familiar or unfamiliar order in familiar tonalities and meters. In inference learning, students are presented with a combination of familiar and unfamiliar patterns in unfamiliar order in familiar or unfamiliar tonalities and meters. Moreover, students engaged in inference learning are not working with only unfamiliar patterns, tonalities, and meters, but also with new or unfamiliar skills, because the inference skills of generalization, creativity/improvisation, and theoretical understanding are not taught in discrimination learning.

Generalization-aural/oral, verbal, and symbolic

At the generalization-aural/oral level, students determine whether two sets of unfamiliar patterns sound the same or different. At the generalization-verbal level, students learn to make judgments about tonality and meter through musical context by audiating series of tonal patterns and rhythm patterns. At the reading sublevel of generalization-symbolic, students are expected to read without assistance (thoughtlessly but habitually called sight reading) one or more familiar and unfamiliar tonal patterns or familiar and unfamiliar rhythm patterns and to identify tonality and meter they are audiating as they read. The writing sublevel of generalization-symbolic works similarly to the reading sublevel.

Creativity/Improvisation-aural/oral and symbolic

Creativity/improvisation has two sublevels: aural/oral and symbolic. Further, creativity/improvisation-symbolic, has two sublevels: reading and writing. There is no verbal sublevel at the creativity/improvisation level because after students complete the verbal association level in discrimination learning, the use of tonal syllables and rhythm syllables to identify patterns, tonalities, and meters becomes another technique to aid in inference learning. Thus, verbal association is unique in music learning theory because it serves both as a level of learning in discrimination learning and a technique in inference learning. One does not create or improvise tonal syllables or rhythm syllables at the creativity/improvisation level. Apart from sound of patterns, syllables have no musical meaning.

At the reading sublevel of creativity/improvisation-symbolic, students learn to read chord symbols or figured bass and perform tonal patterns corresponding to symbols, using either a neutral syllable or tonal syllables. Students learn to recognize or identify tonality they are audiating as they are reading symbols. There is no rhythm component for the reading sublevel. At the writing sublevel of creativity/improvisation-symbolic, students write, rather than perform, in response to tonal patterns and rhythm patterns they are given. The symbolic association and composite synthesis levels of discrimination learning and the generalization-symbolic and creativity/improvisation-aural/oral levels of inference learning all provide direct readiness for the creativity/improvisation-symbolic level of learning.

Theoretical Understanding-aural, verbal, and symbolic

Theoretical understanding has three sublevels: aural/oral, verbal, and symbolic. Theoretical understanding-symbolic has two sublevels: reading and writing. Whereas tonal syllables and rhythm syllables serve as techniques at the verbal association level of discrimination learning, note letter-names, time-value names, interval names, key-signature names, and measure-signature names, for example, which must necessarily be taught by rote, serve as techniques at the theoretical understanding level of inference learning. Students use them to theorize about music after they are able to audiate. In theoretical understanding, only implicit elements of patterns and series of patterns are of concern.

Learning Sequence Activities

Though you may be enthusiastic about benefits that will accrue as a result of your students engaging in learning sequence activities, remember exchanging the familiar for the unfamiliar is a difficult process for you and even more so for students. To be worthwhile, all change is undertaken gradually. Thus, for you to make an abrupt transition from common-practice music theory to learning sequence activities is not recommended. To be worthwhile, change must be undertaken gradually. Rapid change seldom endures.

In the beginning, spend relatively little class time on learning sequence activities, the bulk of attention being on your heretofore customary routine. As time passes, more and more time will naturally be devoted to learning sequence activities as you and your students become conscious of the musical value of what is being absorbed. What you have previously taught them or what they have been taught by others is not to be discarded because it involves terminology needed to communicate with musicians who are not familiar with music learning theory and learning sequence activities. Learning sequence activities contribute to students' musicianship as a result of a better understanding of what they have already been taught. They will find it captivating to be able to associate sound of ongoing music without calling upon note letter-names and time-value names, intervals, and other theoretical terminology that have had little practical meaning for them. Nonetheless, emphasize to students it would be counterproductive for them to revert to familiar definitions to attempt to understand what you are teaching. Simply retaining in reserve what they have been taught in the past for future use is sufficient.

Music Aptitudes

Administration of a music aptitude test is necessary to provide you with knowledge concerning musical potential of individual students so you may effectively teach them tonal patterns and rhythm patterns. That is, test results will guide you in efficiently teaching to individual musical differences among your students. When students' individual musical needs are taken into account, those with limited potential will not become frustrated and those with exceptional potential will not become bored. For college and university students, the *Advanced Measures of Music Audiation* is appropriate. Information pertaining to this and other tests may be found in my book, *Introduction to Research and the Psychology of Music* It is listed in the Bibliography.

Tonal Patterns

The range of tonal patterns used in learning sequence activities is typically less than an octave and rarely more than an octave, the octave being from D above middle C to D above. The tessitura is a major sixth, from D above middle C to B♭ above. If keyality of patterns is inappropriate for your students, transpose but remember, the initial lower limit for musically inexperienced and/or unchanged voices should not go below D above middle C. However, if keyality of at least one of the three patterns is transposed, then keyality of all patterns is transposed. That is, all patterns are taught in the same keyality. The octave may be changed but tonality of patterns may not.

Tonal Sequence

Before students hear or are asked to respond to the majority of tonal patterns in the *Tonal Register Book*, you will have established tonality and keyality in which patterns are to be performed. That is accomplished by singing a tonal sequence (see the following page) usually performed more than once, depending on how many times it is necessary for students to audiate the intended tonality and keyality. The tonal sequence is sung at double the tempo of the individual, dialogue, and class patterns. Students do not sing the sequence with you or after you. Thus, you gesture to students you are performing the tonal sequence and they are only to audiate the tonal sequence. In instances when directions for a criterion do not include a tonal sequence, be sure not to use one.

The name of the tonality to be established with the tonal sequence is written above the notated patterns in the *Tonal Register Book*. *Major* means you sing the tonal sequence in major tonality; *Minor*, in harmonic minor tonality; *Dorian*, in Dorian tonality; and *Mixolydian*, in Mixolydian tonality. The keyality to be established is determined by looking at the name of the tonality and at the key signature on the staff. For example, *Major* in association with two sharps means you sing the tonal sequence in D major, *Minor* in association with one flat means you sing the tonal sequence in D harmonic minor, *Dorian* in association with two sharps means you sing the tonal sequence in E Dorian, and *Mixolydian* in association with one sharp means you sing the tonal sequence in D Mixolydian.

When directions include use of a neutral syllable, sing *bum* or a combination of no more than a few neutral syllables. When directions include use of tonal syllables, movable-*do* syllables with a *do* based major, *la* based minor, *re* based Dorian, and *so* based Mixolydian are sung. Depending on tonality to be established, sing unaccompanied (an instrument, particularly the piano, should not be used), in a comfortable consistent tempo and a musical manner, one of the tonal sequences illustrated below with movable-*do* syllables. A line above a syllable indicates the syllable ascends and a line below means it descends. I recommend you take a reference pitch from a well-tuned instrument, preferably a small and soft-sounding pocket electronic instrument, before singing the tonal sequence.

Note-letter names, though never sung in a tonal sequence, are given below only for your clarification. They are not used with students. Consider a key signature of no sharps or flats. Note letter-names for the tonal sequence in major tonality and C keyality are G A G F E D B C; for harmonic minor tonality and A keyality, E F E D C B G# A; for Dorian tonality and D keyality, A B A G F E C D; and for Mixolydian tonality and G keyality, D E D C B A F G.

Major	so $\overline{\text{la}}$ $\underline{\text{so}}$ $\underline{\text{fa}}$ $\underline{\text{mi}}$ $\underline{\text{re}}$ $\underline{\text{ti}}$ $\overline{\text{do}}$
Harmonic Minor	mi $\overline{\text{fa}}$ $\underline{\text{mi}}$ $\underline{\text{re}}$ $\underline{\text{do}}$ $\underline{\text{ti}}$ $\underline{\text{si}}$ $\overline{\text{la}}$
Dorian	la $\overline{\text{ti}}$ $\underline{\text{la}}$ $\underline{\text{so}}$ $\underline{\text{fa}}$ $\underline{\text{mi}}$ $\underline{\text{do}}$ $\overline{\text{re}}$
Mixolydian	re $\overline{\text{mi}}$ $\underline{\text{re}}$ $\underline{\text{do}}$ $\underline{\text{ti}}$ $\underline{\text{la}}$ $\underline{\text{fa}}$ $\overline{\text{so}}$

Class Patterns

Class patterns are always sung by you and all students in ensemble, in contrast to individual patterns sung by you and one student together (in duet) in the teaching mode and then the student alone (solo) in the evaluation mode.

Purpose of Class Patterns

Class patterns and individual patterns have different purposes. Individual patterns teach students to audiate a pattern vocabulary. Class patterns do not. Class patterns are used to reinforce, maintain, and, if necessary, re-establish tonality and keyality in which individual patterns are being sung, they prevent one student from imitating what another has just sung, they reduce anxiety that might develop among students if individual patterns were sung continuously, and they provide necessary variety. For example, if a succession of tonic individual patterns are sung, then a dominant class pattern is interspersed among them, and vice versa. That sustains the tonality students are audiating.

Determining Which Class Patterns to Use

Class patterns are not notated in the *Register Books*. The reason is the nature of class patterns is relatively unimportant provided they are in the same tonality and keyality as individual patterns and they follow the functions of individual patterns. With regard to pattern functions, it would not make sense to use subdominant class patterns if only tonic and dominant individual patterns are to be performed. On the other hand, all functions of individual patterns need not be used as class patterns.

Initially, learn at least two class patterns in major and harmonic minor tonalities that may be used repeatedly. For major and harmonic minor tonalities, one of the class patterns should be a tonic function pattern (for example, any combination of *do mi so* in major) and the other a dominant function pattern (for example, any combination of *so ti re fa* in major). In major tonality, a tonic pattern may be *do mi* and a dominant pattern *so ti re*. Students learn to audiate tonality sooner if the dominant class pattern includes the leading tone (*ti* for major and *si* for harmonic minor). In harmonic minor tonality, a tonic pattern may be *la do* and a dominant pattern may be *mi ti si*. In Mixolydian tonality, a tonic pattern may be *so ti* and a subtonic pattern may be *fa la do*. In Dorian tonality a tonic pattern may be *re fa*; a subtonic pattern; *do mi so*, and a subdominant pattern, *re so ti*. There is space provided on each page of the *Register Book* to insert, if necessary, notation of class patterns.

You may, of course, use class patterns other than the examples. Naturally you will learn additional patterns as you continue to teach learning sequence activities. Individual patterns used in earlier units typically are used as class patterns in later units. When you are ready to create your own class patterns, use at least two functions that have different numbers of pitches. Most should include two or three pitches (not fewer than two or more than five). All pitches in a tonal pattern should be of the same length. When pitches are of different lengths, they do not establish rhythm or meter, and that is how it should be.

Techniques for Using Class Patterns

If individual patterns are sung using *bum*, class patterns are sung using *bum* unless other directions are given in the *Register Book*, and if individual patterns are sung using tonal syllables, class patterns are sung using tonal syllables unless other directions are given in the *Register Book*. Class patterns are sung at the same tempo by you and students and they are in the same tonality and keyality as individual patterns. If, for example, directions indicate a student is to sing only the first pitch or resting tone of an individual pattern, you follow the same routine with class patterns. Most directions in learning sequence activities include the use of class patterns. When not directed to use class patterns, take care not use them.

Sing at least one or two class patterns before singing individual patterns, but do not sing so many class patterns that too little time is left for students to sing individual patterns for teaching and evaluation purposes. Alternate between singing class patterns and individual patterns. Usually no more than three individual patterns are performed without performing a class pattern.

Class patterns and individual patterns are performed much the same way. Sing the class pattern and pause for a moment or two. Then gesture to students to take a deep breath and quickly make another gesture for them to sing the class pattern in ensemble. The first gesture indicates to students to breathe and the second when to begin singing. A pause must be long enough so students can take in an appropriate amount of breath for audiation purposes and short enough so they will not attempt to memorize a class pattern in actual (real) time. The length of pauses between class patterns need not be the same. The lack of uniformity in the length of pauses assists in not allowing establishment of meter and rhythm. You may or may not, as you wish, sing class patterns with students, singing some but not others.

The momentary pause followed by a deep breath is crucial. The pause prevents imitation, gives students time to audiate patterns within a tonality, and helps keep patterns void of rhythm. By breathing beforehand, students audiate patterns in the proper tonality and sing with good intonation. Audiation takes place during the breath, as students generalize and summarize what they are going to sing before they sing.

Without taking a deep breath, students tend to engage in echoic responses, that is, they simply imitate patterns without audiating them. Some directions indicate you are to perform two or more class patterns in succession. You must make a pause and take a breath after each one. The class also sings a series of class patterns with pauses and breaths between them.

Gesturing is best using hands, body, and face, always with as much weight as your body will comfortably allow. The less talking you do in learning sequence activities, the better. Talking will interrupt your and your students' audiation processes. You might practice alone using gestures with random patterns and then later with the class before using the *Register Book*. Discover which gestures are most comfortable. Once decisions are made, be consistent with those gestures.

Dialogue Patterns

As with class patterns, dialogue patterns reinforce, maintain, and re-establish tonality and keyality. They also prevent imitation and reduce anxiety. Sometimes dialogue patterns are used in place of class patterns. After you sing one or more dialogue patterns (singing out loud to yourself), move directly to an individual pattern without the class responding to the dialogue pattern. Among other virtues, dialogue patterns save time because students do not perform them. That allows more time for learning individual patterns. Dialogue patterns are more practical than class patterns when students read and write patterns.

Individual Tonal Patterns

Audiation of individual patterns is the essence of learning sequence activities. When students sing solo (individual patterns), they learn to audiate. When students sing in ensemble (class patterns), they tend to imitate one another. Of course, students need to learn to imitate before they can learn how to audiate. However, students who continually imitate and memorize may never learn to audiate.

Techniques for Individual Tonal Patterns

As with class tonal patterns, individual tonal patterns are sung with breaths and pauses and without rhythm or meter. They are not accompanied with instruments, especially piano.

All students sing individual patterns in the teaching mode with you in duet and then in the evaluation mode solo. The easy pattern (E) is taught first. After a student learns the easy pattern, the student is taught the moderately difficult pattern (M). After a student learns the moderately difficult pattern, the student learns the difficult pattern (D).

All students, regardless of whether they have high or average tonal aptitude, sing easy and average patterns solo. Unless a pattern is performed solo, it will not become part of a student's audiation vocabulary and thus, it will not serve in higher levels of learning.

Students with high tonal aptitude are expected to learn the E, M, and D patterns. Students with average tonal aptitude are expected to learn the E and M patterns. Students with low tonal aptitude are expected to learn the E pattern. Turn the page in the *Register Book* when approximately 4 out of 5 (80 percent) of students have met their potential.

During a given span of time, students with high tonal aptitude will be performing the easy, moderately difficult, and difficult individual patterns while students with average tonal aptitude will be performing only the easy and moderately difficult individual patterns and while students with low tonal aptitude are performing only the easy individual pattern. You will spend about the same amount of time with each student regardless of their aptitude levels.

For the most part, students sing what you have sung. Other times, as indicated in the *Register Book*, students listen to you sing individual patterns and speak, read, write, create, or improvise in response.

Remember the following techniques:

— Sing a tonal sequence and some class patterns before teaching individual patterns.
— You and students sing individual patterns at the same tempo.

— Teach individual patterns in much the same way as you teach class patterns. Sing the pattern, pause for a moment, and then indicate to an individual student to take a breath and to sing the individual pattern in duet with you in the teaching mode and then later to sing it solo in the evaluation mode. Do not routinely ask a student to sing a pattern in the evaluation mode immediately after singing it in the teaching mode.

— The brief pause followed by a deep breath is crucial. The pause prevents imitation, the breath encourages audiation, and both keep the tonal patterns void of rhythm and meter.

— Move rapidly in your teaching. If you repeatedly make reference to the *Register Book* for directions and to read tonal patterns during the teaching process, students will become bored and uneasy, and that will, among other things, impede their audiation.

— Be sure to use different gestures for indicating to students whether they will be singing class patterns or individual patterns. Perhaps you may extend two arms out for a class pattern and one arm out for an individual pattern. The first gesture indicates when to breathe and the second when to begin singing. If necessary, demonstrate an exaggerated breath. Gesture using arms, hands, and face, always moving your body parts which carry most weight. Be consistent with your gestures. The less talking you do during learning sequence activities, the better.

— The length of pauses between your and a student's performance of the individual pattern is not uniform. A pause must be long enough to allow the student to take a deep breath and short enough to prevent memorization.

— Sometimes two or more individual patterns are sung in succession. As with class patterns, you and students pause and breathe between individual patterns.

— As little advance notice as possible should be given to the student who will be singing an individual pattern. For example, the gesture to breathe is directed toward one student and the gesture to sing is directed toward another. In that way, all students will be audiating, because any one of them may be asked to sing at any time. By waiting before gesturing to a student to sing an individual pattern, anxiety is significantly reduced.

— A student is not called by name to sing an individual pattern. That creates anxiety and interferes with audiation. Gestures, without pointing, are recommended.

— Do not be too lenient in accepting a less than acceptable performance by a student with high music aptitude. Whether performing an easy, moderately difficult, or difficult pattern, be sure all students are putting forth their best effort. To deny a student with high aptitude ample instruction because it is believed the student is able to teach himself or herself is to do that student an injustice. Under such conditions, the student could become disinterested and achieve less than a motivated student with lower music aptitude. On the other hand, do not lose patience with a student who has low music aptitude. Although it usually takes longer, a student with low aptitude will in time be capable of giving an acceptable performance of at least the easy pattern.

— Should a student with very high tonal aptitude achieve the performance of a difficult pattern in the teaching mode and evaluation modes in a short time and seemingly become bored, ask the student to perform both the easy and moderately difficult patterns in succession. As a further challenge, ask the student to perform the easy, moderately difficult, and difficult patterns in succession and/or in different orders.

— You will find teaching most efficient and enjoyable when it is not necessary to read directions or notation in the *Register Book*. Of course, occasional reference to directions and notation is to be expected. Enthusiastic facial expressions and continuous eye-to-eye contact with students is especially valuable when teaching learning sequence activities.

— Skill, tonal context, and tonal content are titled on each page in the *Register Book* under the notated tonal patterns. Skill level is in capital letters to the left and tonal content and context to the right. Specific detailed techniques (more abundant than those given in the *Register Books*) for teaching all tonal units are outlined in sequential order in the *Reference Handbook for Teaching Learning Sequence Activities*.

Rhythm Patterns

Unique concepts are used to teach rhythm in learning sequence activities. Explanations associated with common-practice music theory are avoided. If you are not familiar with the preferred information or for review, I suggest you read my book, *Learning Sequences in Music: A Contemporary Music Learning Theory*. For an immediate, although brief, introduction, refer to Part 4 in this book and read the section between suggestions 9 and 10 under Rhythm Development. There you will find an explication of rhythm in terms of macrobeats, microbeats, and rhythm patterns and their relation to measure signatures. Also, see Melody 23 in Part 1 of this book for a description of beat-function rhythm solfege in verbal and notation form. Rhythm patterns are explained and notated in terms of their functions in Part 3 of this book under Rhythm Development.

Rhythm Sequence

Before students hear or are asked to respond to the majority of patterns in the *Rhythm Register Book*, you will have established meter and tempo in which patterns are to be performed. That is accomplished by chanting a rhythm sequence that may be performed more than once, depending on how many times it is necessary for students to audiate the intended meter and tempo. The rhythm sequence is chanted at the tempo class patterns, dialogue patterns, and individual patterns are performed. A pause is made between repeated performances of the rhythm sequence. The pause may be the length of any number of macrobeats. Each time the rhythm sequence is performed, however, it must begin on a macrobeat. To achieve that, you continually audiate macrobeats during the pauses. Chant a rhythm sequence with rhythm syllables or the neutral syllable *bah* (or a combination of no more than a few neutral syllables) as indicated in the directions in the *Rhythm*

Register Book. Whether using *bah* or rhythm syllables, chant with expressive inflections. The same pitch, however, is used for all durations.

Following are recommended rhythm sequences.

Usual Duple	*du be du* ǀ *du be da*
Usual Triple	*du da di du* ǀ *du da di du*
Usual Combined	*du de du da di* ǀ *du de du da di*
Unusual Paired	*du be du ba bi* ǀ *du be du ba bi*
Unusual Unpaired	*du be du be du ba bi* ǀ *du be du be du ba bi*

Students do not chant the sequence with you or after you. Thus, gesture to students you are performing the rhythm sequence and they are only to audiate the rhythm sequence. The same gestures for teaching tonal patterns may be used for teaching rhythm patterns. After the rhythm sequence is performed the last time, there must be a pause of two macrobeats (no more, no less) before the first class pattern or individual pattern is performed. In instances when directions do not include a rhythm sequence, take care not to use one.

The name of the meter to be established with the rhythm sequence is written above the notated patterns in the *Register Book*. *Usual Duple* means you chant the rhythm sequence in usual duple meter; *Usual Triple*; in usual triple meter; *Usual Combined*, in usual combined meter; *Unusual Paired*, in unusual paired meter; and *Unusual Unpaired*, in unusual unpaired meter. In usual combined, unusual paired, and unusual unpaired meters, the order of microbeats performed in the rhythm sequence may not be the same as the order of the underlying groupings of microbeats in the class patterns and individual patterns. That presents no difficulty.

Tempo of the rhythm sequence should be comfortable for you and students. Although tempo need not be the same for all meters or the same from day-to-day for any one meter, it must be kept consistent for all patterns on a given day. Use your discretion in establishing tempo. Tempos too slow are boring and tempos too fast may make rhythm patterns unnecessarily difficult, if not impossible, to perform accurately. As a general rule, usual triple meter is performed slightly slower than usual duple meter. Perhaps you may find it helpful to use a small electronic instrument to establish appropriate tempos.

Sometimes one or more rhythm patterns are performed in succession, but collectively they are considered one rhythm pattern. No pauses are made between them. Typically, class, dialogue, and individual patterns in learning sequence activities are at least four macrobeats in length in all three usual meters. In unusual paired meter, class, dialogue, and individual patterns are at least two macrobeats in length. In unusual unpaired meter, class, dialogue, and individual patterns are at least three macrobeats in length.

Class Patterns

Class patterns are always chanted by you and all students in ensemble, in contrast to individual patterns chanted first by you and one student together (in duet) in the teaching mode, and then by the student solo in the evaluation mode.

Purpose of Class Patterns

Class patterns and individual patterns play different roles. Individual patterns teach students how to audiate. Class patterns do not. Class patterns are used to reinforce, maintain, and, if necessary, re-establish the meter and tempo in which individual patterns are chanted. Also, class patterns prevent immediate imitation from one student to another, they reduce anxiety that might develop among students if individual patterns were chanted continuously, and they provide necessary variety. For example, if a succession of macro/microbeat individual patterns are chanted, then a division class pattern should be interspersed among them, and vice versa. That sustains the meter students are audiating.

Determining Which Class Patterns to Use

Class patterns are not notated in the *Register Book*. The reason is the nature of class patterns used is relatively unimportant, provided they are in the same meter and tempo as individual patterns and they follow the functions of individual patterns. With regard to pattern functions, it would not make sense to use division class patterns if only macro/microbeat individual patterns are to be performed. On the other hand, all functions of individual patterns in a unit need not be used as class patterns. Patterns are chanted at the same tempo by you and students and they are in the same meter and tempo as individual patterns. It is best when class patterns and individual patterns have the same number of underlying macrobeats and are chanted with inflection and expression. All durations in a rhythm pattern, however, should be without pitch. There is space provided on each page of the *Rhythm Registers Book* to insert, if necessary, notation of class patterns.

Initially, learn at least one macro/microbeat pattern and one division pattern in usual duple, usual triple, and usual combined meters. For example, in usual duple meter, *du du | du de du* and *du du ta de ta | du de du*. In usual triple meter, *du du | du da di du* and *du ta da ta di ta du | du da di du*. In usual combined meter, *du de du | du da di du* and *du ta de ta du | du ta da ta di ta du*. Later, for unusual paired meter, *du be du ba bi | du du* and *du ta be ta du | du ta ba ta bi ta du*. For unusual unpaired meter, *du be du be du ba bi | du be du ba bi du* and *du ta be ta du ba bi | du ta ba ta bi ta du*.

You may and are, of course, encouraged to use class patterns other than those suggested. Naturally you will learn additional patterns as you continue to teach learning sequence activities. Individual patterns used in earlier units typically are used as class patterns in later units. When you are ready to create your own class patterns, use macro/microbeat patterns in usual duple meter and usual triple meters. Use macro/microbeat and division patterns in usual combined meter, unusual paired meter, and unusual unpaired meter.

Techniques for Using Class Patterns

If individual patterns are chanted using *bah*, class patterns are chanted using *bah* unless other directions are given, and if individual patterns are chanted using rhythm syllables, class patterns are chanted using rhythm syllables unless other directions are given. Most directions in learning sequence activities include the use of class patterns. When not directed to use class patterns, take care not use them.

Chant at least one or two class patterns before chanting individual patterns, but do not chant so many class patterns that too little time is left to chant an appropriate number of individual patterns for teaching and evaluation purposes. Alternate between chanting class patterns and individual patterns. No more than three individual patterns are performed without performing a class pattern.

Rhythm patterns are performed the same way as tonal patterns with one exception: Pauses are not made between class patterns and between individual patterns. The only pause comes between repeated performances of the rhythm sequence and after the final performance. Pauses are not necessary because students are aware of the meter (context) as a result of audiating underlying macrobeats and microbeat. Moreover, if pauses are made, meter and tempo become imprecise and inconsistent.

Although there are no pauses once the chanting of class patterns begins, students are gestured to breathe so they will be able to audiate the class pattern before they chant it. Students take a breath on the final macrobeat of your performance of the class pattern. Sometimes you will need to gesture on the final macrobeat while you are still chanting a class pattern. During the breath, students generalize and summarize in audiation the class pattern you are chanting and they will soon chant.

After you chant a class pattern (usually four underlying macrobeats in length in usual meter), students chant that class pattern beginning on the next macrobeat (usually on the fifth underlying macrobeat in usual meter) which immediately follows the fourth macrobeat of the class pattern. After students chant a class pattern, you chant another class pattern beginning on the next macrobeat immediately following the final macrobeat of the class pattern the students chanted.

The same gestures used with tonal patterns, except for the pause, are used for rhythm patterns. Use one gesture to indicate to students to breathe on the last macrobeat of the class pattern and another gesture to indicate to students to begin chanting on the following macrobeat. Arms, hands, body, and face, using as much body weight as possible while moving without conducting, are used in gesturing with as little talking as possible. Talking will interrupt your and students' audiation processes. You might practice alone using gestures with random patterns and then later with the class before using the *Register Book*. Discover which gestures are most comfortable. Once decisions are made, be consistent with those gestures.

Dialogue Patterns

Like class patterns, dialogue patterns reinforce, maintain, and re-establish meter and tempo. They also prevent imitation and reduce anxiety. Sometimes dialogue patterns are used in place of class patterns. After chanting one or more dialogue patterns (chanting out loud to yourself), move directly to an individual pattern without the class responding to the dialogue pattern. Among other virtues, dialogue patterns save time because students do not perform them. That allows more time for individual patterns. Dialogue patterns serve much better than class patterns particularly when students are directed to read and write patterns.

Individual Rhythm Patterns

Audiation of individual patterns is the essence of learning sequence activities. When students chant solo (individual patterns), they learn to audiate. When students chant in ensemble (class patterns), they tend to imitate one another. Of course, students learn to imitate before they learn how to audiate. However, students who continually imitate and memorize may never learn to audiate.

Techniques for Individual Patterns

Individual rhythm patterns are chanted on the same pitch. However, they are chanted with inflection and expression, as if being used in conversation.

All students chant the individual patterns in the teaching mode with you in duet and then in the evaluation mode solo. The easy pattern (E) is taught first. After a student learns the easy pattern, the student is taught the moderately difficult pattern (M). After a student learns the moderately difficult pattern, the student learns the difficult pattern (D).

Students with high rhythm aptitude are expected to learn the E, M, and D patterns. Students with average rhythm aptitude are expected to learn the E and M patterns. Students with low rhythm aptitude are expected to learn the E pattern. Turn the page in the *Register Book* when approximately 4 out of 5 (80 percent) of students have met their potential.

Regardless of whether they have high or average rhythm aptitude, all students learn the easy and moderately difficult patterns. Unless a pattern is performed solo, it will not become part of a student's audiation vocabulary and thus, it will not serve for learning higher levels of learning.

During a given span of time, students with high rhythm aptitude will be performing the easy, moderately difficult, and difficult individual patterns while students with average rhythm aptitude will be performing only the easy and moderately difficult individual patterns and while students with low rhythm aptitude are performing only the easy individual pattern. You will spend about the same amount of time with each student, regardless of their aptitude levels.

For the most part, students chant what you have chanted. Other times, as indicated in the *Register Book*, students listen to you chant individual patterns and speak, read, write, create, and improvise in response.

Remember the following techniques:

- — Chant the appropriate rhythm sequence and some class patterns before teaching individual patterns.
- — You and students chant individual patterns at the same tempo.
- — Teach the individual patterns in much the same way as you teach class patterns. Pauses are not made when teaching individual rhythm patterns.
- — After you chant an individual pattern (usually four macrobeats in length), students chant that individual pattern beginning on the next macrobeat (usually the fifth macrobeat) which immediately follows the fourth macrobeat of the class pattern. After students chant an individual pattern, you chant another

individual pattern beginning on the next macrobeat immediately following the final macrobeat of the individual pattern the students chanted.

— Move rapidly in your teaching. If you repeatedly make reference to the *Register Book* for directions and to read rhythm patterns during the teaching process, students will become bored and uneasy, and that will, among other things, impede their audiation.

— Although there are no pauses once the chanting of patterns begin, students need to be told when to breathe so they will audiate the pattern before they perform it. The student should take a breath on the final macrobeat of your pattern. Use a gesture to tell the student when to breath. During the breath, the student audiates the pattern to be chanted. If necessary, demonstrate an exaggerated breath. Gesture using your arms, hands, and face, always moving your body parts which carry most weight. Be consistent with your gestures. The less talking you do during learning sequence activities, the better.

— Sometimes two or more individual patterns are chanted in succession. As with class patterns, do not pause between individual patterns.

— As little advance notice as possible should be given to the student who will be chanting the individual pattern. For example, the gesture to breathe is directed toward one student and the gesture to chant is directed toward another. In that way, all students will be audiating, because any one of them may be asked to chant at any time. By waiting before gesturing to a student to chant an individual pattern, anxiety is significantly reduced. Should anxiety arise even when using that procedure, only class patterns should be used until the students appear to be comfortable.

— A student is not called by name to chant an individual pattern. That creates anxiety and interferes with audiation. Gestures, without pointing, are recommended.

— Do not be too lenient in accepting a less than acceptable performance by a student with high music aptitude. Whether performing an easy, moderately difficult, or difficult pattern, be sure all students are putting forth their best effort. To deny a student with high aptitude ample instruction because it is believed the student is able to teach himself or herself is to do that student an injustice. Under such conditions, the student could become disinterested and achieve less than a student with lower music aptitude. On the other hand, do not lose patience with a student who has low music aptitude. Although it usually takes longer, a student with low aptitude will in time be capable of giving an acceptable performance of the easy pattern.

— Should a student with very high rhythm aptitude achieve the performance of a difficult pattern in the teaching mode and evaluation mode in a short amount of time and seemingly become bored, ask the student to perform both the easy and moderately difficult pattern in succession. As a further challenge, ask the student to perform the easy, moderately difficult, and difficult patterns in succession and/or in different orders.

— You will find teaching most efficient and enjoyable when it is not necessary for you to read directions or notation in the *Register Book*. Of course, occasional reference to directions and notation is to be expected. Enthusiastic facial expressions and continuous eye-to-eye contact with students is especially valuable when using learning sequence activities.

— Skill, rhythm context, and rhythm content are titled on each page in the *Register Book* under the notated rhythm patterns. The skill level is in capital letters to the left and rhythm content and context is to the right. Specific detailed techniques (more abundant than those given in the *Register Books*) for teaching all rhythm units are outlined in sequential order in the *Reference Handbook for Teaching Learning Sequence Activities*.

Register Books and Record Keeping

As explained in the *Reference Handbook for Using Learning Sequence Activities*, a Unit number, Section letter, and Criterion number are indicated at the top of each page under the notated patterns in *Tonal*

Register Books One and *Two and Rhythm Register Books One* and *Two*. Also, there is a Seating/Evaluation Chart on each page. Every chart includes forty-eight boxes. According to where they are seated in the classroom, individual student names and music aptitude test results are written in each box. Students who score high (80th percentile and above) have a line above their name, and students who score low (20th percentile and below) have a line below their name. No line is drawn for students whose score is average (from the 21st to 79th percentile). Information on the chart need not be rewritten on each page of the *Register Books* when a master chart is organized at the beginning of instruction and multiple duplicates are made on a copy machine. Then, duplicates are pasted over each blank seating chart. Of course, individual student's music aptitude test results will be different on Seating/Evaluation charts in *Tonal Register Books* and *Rhythm Register Books*.

An immediate record is made on the Seating/Evaluation Chart of each student's performance of solo patterns in the teaching and evaluation modes. In the teaching mode, you sing or chant in duet with the student. As you and the student sing, you listen carefully to determine if the student is reasonably capable of singing or chanting the pattern. If so, the next time the student is asked to sing or chant the solo pattern you give a familiar gesture indicating you will perform in duet again as you did before in the teaching mode. However, this time you remain silent as the student performs solo in the evaluation mode. If you decide after either the teaching mode or evaluation mode the student still requires your assistance, you continue performing with the student in the teaching mode until you are given evidence the student is ready to perform solo successfully in the evaluation mode.

When a student performs the easy pattern acceptably in the teaching mode, a single vertical line is made in the appropriate box on the Seating/Evaluation Chart. By marking the box, you will know the next time you gesture to the student he or she is to perform the easy pattern solo in the evaluation mode. When the student successfully performs the easy pattern in the evaluation mode, the single line is crossed. By looking at the Seating/Evaluation Chart it can be quickly discerned the next time you gesture to the student to perform a pattern it will be the moderately difficult pattern in the teaching mode. Then the student will perform the moderately difficult pattern in the evaluation mode. At that time there will be two crossed lines in the student's box. The process is repeated for the difficult pattern and then there will be three crossed lines in the box.

Depending upon a student's musical potential as indicated by music aptitude test results, there may be no lines or from one vertical line to three crossed lines in each box. Keeping such records provides for thoughtful and precise instruction during the school year that is not wasteful of time and energy and takes into account students' individual musical needs in terms of their individual musical differences.

Glossary

Aeolian Tonality	Tonality of *la* to *la* with *la* as the resting tone. When compared to harmonic minor tonality, it has a lowered seventh-step.
Audiation	Hearing and comprehending in one's mind sound of music not, or may never have been, physically present. It is not imitation or memorization. There are six stages of audiation and eight types of audiation.
Aural/Oral	First (most elementary) level of discrimination learning and foundation for all other levels of discrimination learning and inference learning. At this level of learning students use a neutral syllable to imitate tonal patterns and rhythm patterns.
Aural Perception	Hearing music when sound is physically present.
Bridging Movement	Temporary skipping of one or more sequential skill, tonal, and rhythm levels of learning in learning sequence activities.
Cadential Pattern	One function of tonal patterns. A cadential pattern is found at the end of a series of tonal patterns.

Characteristic-Tone Pattern	One function of tonal patterns. Every tonality includes one or more characteristic tones. For example, in Mixolydian tonality, a characteristic-tone pattern includes a lowered-seventh as compared to major tonality. In Dorian tonality, a characteristic-tone pattern includes one or both a raised sixth-step and lowered seventh-step as compared to harmonic minor tonality.
Chromatic Pattern	One function of tonal patterns. A chromatic pattern includes one or more chromatic pitches.
Chromatics	See movable *do* syllables.
Chord	Four or more pitches sounded simultaneously.
Class Patterns	Patterns a class performs in ensemble during learning sequence activities.
Composite Synthesis-reading	Highest (most advanced) level of discrimination learning. At this level of learning, students learn to read comprehensively, using tonal syllables and rhythm syllables, series of tonal patterns and series of rhythm patterns taught at lower levels of learning.
Composite Synthesis-writing	Highest (most advanced) level of discrimination learning. At this level of learning, students learn to notate comprehensively, using tonal syllables and rhythm syllables, series of tonal patterns and series of rhythm patterns taught at lower levels of learning.
Content	Tonal patterns and rhythm patterns that constitute a piece of music.
Context	Tonality and meter of music that comprise component patterns of a piece of music.
Creativity	Spontaneous audiation and use of tonal patterns and rhythm patterns without restrictions.

Creativity/ Improvisation-aural/oral	One level of inference learning. Creativity/ improvisation takes place with verbal association (using tonal syllables to perform tonal patterns and rhythm syllables to perform rhythm patterns) or without verbal association (using a neutral syllable to perform tonal patterns and to perform rhythm patterns). At this level of learning students create and improvise using familiar patterns, those imitated in discrimination learning, and unfamiliar patterns.
Curriculum	Sequential presentation of progressively complex skills and knowledge.
Developmental Music Aptitude	Music potential affected by the quality of environmental factors. A child is in the developmental music aptitude stage from birth to approximately nine years old.
Dialogue Patterns	Used in place of class patterns. Students listen but do not perform.
Discrimination Learning	Lower of two generic types of skill learning. In discrimination learning students are taught skills and patterns through imitation. Discrimination learning includes aural/oral, verbal association, partial synthesis, symbolic association-reading, symbolic association-writing, composite synthesis-reading, and composite synthesis-writing. Discrimination learning is readiness for inference learning.
Division Pattern	One function of rhythm patterns. A division pattern includes a division of a microbeat (a duration shorter than a microbeat) or a division of a macrobeat (a duration shorter than a macrobeat but not a microbeat).

Division/ Elongation Pattern	One function of rhythm patterns. A division/ elongation pattern includes an elongation of a microbeat (a duration longer than a microbeat but not a macrobeat) and/or an elongation of a macrobeat (a duration longer than a macrobeat) or a division of a microbeat (a duration shorter than a microbeat) and/or a division of a macrobeat (a duration shorter than a macrobeat but not a microbeat).
"Do" Signature	Traditionally called key signature. However, it does not indicate any one tonality or keyality. It does indicate where *do* is found on the staff.
Dominant-Seventh Pattern	One function of tonal patterns. For example, in major tonality it includes an arrangement of *so ti re fa*.
Dorian Tonality	Tonality of *re* to *re* with *re* as the resting tone. When compared to harmonic minor tonality, it has a raised sixth-step and lowered seventh-step.
Duple Meter	See usual duple meter.
Duration	Part of a rhythm pattern. For example, each eighth-note in a rhythm pattern of two eighth-notes is a duration.
Elongation Pattern	One function of rhythm patterns. An elongation pattern includes an elongation of a microbeat (a duration longer than a microbeat but not a macrobeat) or an elongation of a macrobeat (a duration longer than a macrobeat).
Enharmonic	Tonal patterns that sound the same but are notated differently. Also, key signatures used to notate the same sounding keyality.
Enrhythmic	Rhythm patterns that sound the same but are notated differently. Also, measure signatures used to notate the same sounding meter. Enrhythmic is to rhythm notation and audiation what enharmonic is to tonal notation and audiation.

Evaluation Mode	When a teacher does not sing or chant with a student as the student performs an individual pattern solo in learning sequence activities.
Expanded Pattern	One function of tonal patterns. In major tonality it includes patterns based on supertonic (*re fa la*), mediant (*mi so ti*), submediant (*la do mi*), and leading tone (*ti re fa*).
Familiar Order of Patterns	Patterns taught in specific order in discrimination learning. In discrimination learning students deal with familiar patterns in both familiar or unfamiliar order.
Familiar Patterns	Patterns students learned solo at aural/oral and verbal association levels of discrimination learning.
Functions	Tonal functions in major tonality are tonic, dominant-seventh, subdominant, cadential, chromatic, modulatory, multiple, and expanded patterns. Rhythm functions are macro/microbeat, division, elongation, division/elongation, rest, tie, and upbeat patterns.
Generalization-aural/oral	First (most elementary) level of inference learning. At this and all other levels of inference learning, students audiate familiar and unfamiliar tonal patterns and rhythm patterns in unfamiliar order. The aural/oral level of discrimination learning is direct readinesses for generalization-aural/oral inference learning.
Generalization-symbolic	One level of inference learning. At this level of learning students read and notate familiar and unfamiliar tonal patterns and rhythm patterns in unfamiliar order. The symbolic association and composite synthesis levels of discrimination learning are direct readiness for generalization-symbolic inference learning.

Generalization-verbal	One level of inference learning. At this level of learning students verbally associate and synthesize familiar and unfamiliar tonal patterns and rhythm patterns in unfamiliar order. The verbal association and partial synthesis levels of discrimination learning are direct readiness for generalization-verbal inference learning.
Harmonic Minor Tonality	Tonality of *la* to *la* with *la* as the resting tone. When compared to Aeolian tonality, it has a raised seventh-step. Harmonic minor, not Aeolian, is the basic tonality in learning sequence activities. Melodic minor and both types of Hungarian (Gypsy) minor are variations of harmonic minor tonality.
Harmonic Pattern	Three triads or chords audiated linearly as a unit.
Harmonic Progression	Contiguous harmonic patterns audiated linearly as a unit.
Hungarian Minor	There are two Hungarian minor scales. One is *la li di re mi fa si la* and the other *la ti do ri mi fa si la*.
Identification	Unfamiliar patterns are identified, whereas familiar patterns are recognized. Recognizing patterns in discrimination learning forms the foundation for identifying patterns in inference learning.
Idiographic Evaluation	Comparing students' music achievement to their music aptitude or past music achievement.
Imitation	Repeating music heard but not audiated, that is, without giving it musical meaning. Imitation may be immediate or delayed.
Improvisation	Spontaneous audiation and use of tonal patterns and rhythm patterns with restrictions.
Individual Patterns	Patterns students perform solo in learning sequence activities.

Inference Learning
Higher of two generic types of skill learning. In inference learning students are guided by the teacher to learn skills and tonal and rhythm patterns by teaching themselves. Students are not taught by imitation in inference learning. Inference learning includes generalization-aural/oral, generalization-verbal, generalization-symbolic, creativity/improvisation-aural/oral, creativity/ improvisation-symbolic, theoretical understanding-aural/oral, theoretical understanding-verbal, and theoretical understanding-symbolic.

Instrumental Activities
Traditional activities in band and orchestra rehearsals and beginning instrumental music classes coordinated with, but separate from, learning sequence activities.

Intact Macrobeat
Macrobeat in unusual meter not long enough to be divided into microbeats. It can be divided into only one or more divisions of a microbeat. An intact macrobeat is the durational equivalent of a microbeat.

Key Signature
Actually a *do* signature. A key signature is seen in notation, whereas keyality is audiated. A key signature does not indicate any one keyality. For example, the key signature of three flats may indicate E♭ keyality in major tonality, C keyality in harmonic minor or Aeolian tonality, F keyality in Dorian tonality, G keyality in Phrygian tonality, A♭ keyality in Lydian tonality, B♭ keyality in Mixolydian tonality, and D keyality in Locrian tonality. Nevertheless, although *do* is not the resting tone in all those tonalities, E♭ is *do* in all of them.

Keyality
Pitch name of the tonic. Keyality is audiated, whereas a key signature is seen in notation. C is the keyality in C major, in C harmonic minor, in C Aeolian, in C Dorian, in C Phrygian, and so on. Tonic is associated with keyality, whereas resting tone is associated with tonality.

Leading-Tone Pattern	One function of tonal patterns. A leading-tone pattern in major tonality, for example, includes an arrangement of *ti re fa*.
Learning Sequence Activities	Activities that include skill learning sequence, tonal and rhythm learning sequences, and pattern learning sequences They take place during the first ten minutes of a class or rehearsal. Tonal and rhythm register books are used by the teacher for learning sequence activities.
Locrian Tonality	Tonality of *ti* to *ti* with *ti* as the resting tone. When compared to harmonic minor tonality, it has a lowered second-step, raised third-step, lowered fifth-step, raised sixth-step, and lowered seventh-step.
Locomotion	Engaging in movement while traveling around a room.
Lydian Tonality	Tonality of *fa* to *fa* with *fa* as resting tone. When compared to major tonality, it has a raised fourth-step.
Macrobeats	Fundamental beats in a rhythm pattern. In usual duple meter in 2/4, quarter notes are performed or are underlying macrobeats. In usual triple meter in 6/8, dotted-quarter notes are performed or are underlying macrobeats. In usual triple meter in 3/4, dotted-half notes are performed or are underlying macrobeats. In unusual meters in 5/8 and 7/8, performed or underlying macrobeats are combinations of quarter notes and dotted-quarter notes.
Macro/Microbeat Pattern	One function of rhythm patterns. A macro/microbeat pattern includes combinations of macrobeats and microbeats, only macrobeats, or only microbeats.

Major Tonality	Tonality of *do* to *do* with *do* as the resting tone. When compared to harmonic minor tonality, it has a raised third-step and raised sixth-step.
Measure Signature	Traditionally called time signature or meter signature. However, measure signatures indicate neither meter nor time, only the fractional values of a whole note found in a measure. Because measure signatures are enrhythmic, a measure signature cannot indicate any one meter. Tempo markings and metronome markings indicate tempo, measure signatures do not.
Mediant Pattern	One function of tonal patterns. For example, a mediant pattern in major tonality includes an arrangement of *mi so ti*.
Melodic Pattern	Combination of a tonal pattern and rhythm pattern.
Memorization	Learning by heart music read or heard, but not necessarily audiated.
Meter	Usual meter is determined by how macrobeats of equal length are divided. There are three types of usual meter. When macrobeats are divided into two microbeats of equal duration, the result is usual duple meter. When macrobeats are divided into three microbeats of equal duration, the result is usual triple meter. When some macrobeats are divided into two and others are divided into three microbeats, and not all microbeats are of equal duration, the result is usual combined meter. Unusual meter is determined by how macrobeats of unequal temporal lengths, some of which may be intact, are grouped. There are four types of unusual meter. They are unusual paired, unusual unpaired, unusual paired intact, and unusual unpaired intact.

Microbeats	Divisions of a macrobeat. The following are examples: In usual duple meter in 2/4, groups of two eighth-notes are performed or are underlying microbeats. In usual triple meter in 6/8, groups of three eighth-notes are performed or are underlying microbeats, or in usual triple meter in 3/4, groups of three quarter-notes are performed or are underlying microbeats. In unusual meters in 5/8 and 7/8, groups of two eighth-notes and groups of three eighth-notes are performed or are underlying microbeats.
Minor Tonality	See harmonic minor tonality.
Mixolydian Tonality	Tonality of *so* to *so* with *so* as the resting tone. When compared to major tonality, it has a lowered seventh step.
Modal	Music not in major or harmonic minor tonality.
Mode	A mode is a tonality. Mode does not mean modal. All tonalities are modes. Major (Ionian mode) and minor (Aeolian mode) are, of course, modes, just as are Dorian and Mixolydian.
Modulatory Pattern	One function of tonal patterns. A modulatory pattern includes a keyality modulation (for example, from C to G), a tonality modulation (for example, from major to harmonic minor), or both (for example, from C major to G harmonic minor).
Movable "do" Syllables	Tonal system in which placement and position of *do* are dependent on keyality. For example, in major tonality, C is *do* in C keyality; D is *do* in D keyality; and so on. Ascending chromatic syllables are *do, di, re, ri, mi, fa, fi, so, si, la, li, ti, do*. Descending chromatic syllables are *do, ti, te, la, le, so, se, fa, mi, me, re, ra, do*. In the immovable or fixed "do" system, regardless of keyality, C is always *do*. The tonal syllable system used in learning sequence activities is movable *do* with a *la* based minor.

Multiple Pattern	One function of tonal patterns. A multiple pattern combines (is a multiple of) two or more harmonic functions (or includes non-harmonic tones). For example, in major tonality with the pattern *do re mi*, *do* and *mi* may belong to tonic function and *re* may belong to dominant-seventh function.
Music Achievement	Accomplishment in musical skills and knowledge.
Music Aptitude	Potential to achieve in music.
Music Learning Theory	Analysis and synthesis of the sequential manner in which we learn music.
Neutral Syllable	A nonsense syllable, rather than tonal syllables or rhythm syllables, used to perform patterns.
Nonlocomotion	Engaging in movement while remaining stationary.
Normative Evaluation	Comparing a student's music aptitude and/or music achievement with the music aptitude and/or music achievement of other students in the same grade or of the same age.
Notational Audiation	Audiation of what is seen in music notation without aid of physical sound.
Note	A symbol read or written in music notation that represents what should be audiated.
Note Letter-Names	Names of lines and spaces of the staff.
Octatonic Scale	Theoretical scale that consists of alternating whole and half-steps. It takes one of two following forms: *do re ri fa fi si la ti do* and *do di ri mi fi so la li do*.
Partial Synthesis	A level of discrimination learning. At this level of learning students audiate tonality of series of familiar tonal patterns and meter of series of familiar rhythm patterns.

Pentatonic	Music that consists of only five tones. Because traditionally it does not include a leading tone, it can only suggest a tonality. The most common pentatonic scale is *do re mi so la*.
Percentile Ranks	Positions derived from raw scores. Because they have standard meaning, they provide for immediate and clear interpretation.
Phrygian Tonality	Tonality of *mi* to *mi* with *mi* as the resting tone. When compared to harmonic minor tonality, it has a lowered second-step and lowered seventh-step.
Pitch Names	Letter names associated with sounds of pitches not seen on the staff.
Proper Names	Names of tonality classifications, tonal functions, meter classifications, and rhythm functions. For example, classification of major and function of tonic, and classification of usual duple and function of macro/microbeats.
Recognition	Familiar patterns are recognized, whereas unfamiliar patterns are identified. Ability to identify unfamiliar patterns in inference learning is based on ability to recognize familiar patterns in discrimination learning.
Record Keeping	Systematic documentation of students' potential and progressive achievement.
Readiness	Background necessary to achieve sequential objectives.
Rest Pattern	One function of rhythm patterns. A rest pattern includes one or more rests.
Resting Tone	Sometimes referred to as a scale tone or home tone. A tonal center or centers to which a piece of music gravitates. A resting tone is specified by a movable *do* syllable in the movable *do* system with a *la* based minor. Tonality has a resting tone, whereas keyality has a tonic.

Rhythm	That which consists of three fundamental parts: macrobeats, microbeats, and rhythm patterns. In audiation, microbeats are superimposed on macrobeats, and rhythm patterns are superimposed on microbeats and macrobeats.
Rhythm Learning Sequence	Rhythm learning sequence includes all rhythm classifications and functions. Classifications and functions are taught sequentially in combination with skill learning sequence.
Rhythm Pattern	Two or more durations in a given meter audiated sequentially and forming a whole.
Rhythm Solfege	See rhythm syllables.
Rhythm Syllables	Different names chanted for different durations in a rhythm pattern. Rhythm syllables used in learning sequence activities are based on beat functions (macrobeats and microbeats) and divisions of beats rather than on time-value names of notes.
Rote Learning	A simple process, characterized by memorization, which requires students remember what they have learned in much the same way it was presented during instruction. Rote learning is useful only at the aural/oral level of music learning theory.
Sequence	Series of pitches or durations sung or chanted by the teacher in learning sequence activities to establish tonality or meter for class, dialogue, and individual tonal patterns and rhythm patterns before being performed by students solo and in ensemble.
Sequential Objective	One in a series of objectives. Once achieved, it serves as readiness for learning the next sequential objective and ultimately, a comprehensive objective in learning sequence activities.

Skill Learning Sequence	Curriculum that includes all discrimination and inference skills taught sequentially to students in conjunction with tonal or rhythm learning sequences.
Sonority	Overall sound resulting from combining two or more distinct sounds. For example, in a chord or choral or instrumental ensemble.
Stabilized Music Aptitude	Music potential no longer affected by environmental factors. One enters the stabilized music aptitude stage at approximately nine years old, and remains there throughout life.
Stepwise Movement	Progression from one level of learning to the next sequential level of learning in learning sequence activities.
Subdominant Pattern	One function of tonal patterns. For example, in major tonality a subdominant pattern includes an arrangement of *fa la do*.
Submediant Pattern	One function of tonal patterns. For example, a submediant pattern in major tonality includes an arrangement of *la do mi*.
Subtonic	A pitch one half-step below the leading tone, which is one whole-step below the tonic. For example, if C is tonic, subtonic is B♭.
Subtonic Pattern	One function of tonal patterns. For example, in Dorian tonality, which has the resting tone *re*, a subtonic pattern includes an arrangement of *do mi so*.
Supertonic Pattern	One function of tonal patterns. For example, a supertonic pattern in major tonality includes an arrangement of *re fa la*.
Syllable Names	Also called vocabulary names in learning sequence activities. An example of syllable names in a tonal pattern is *do so* and in a rhythm pattern is *du ta de ta*.

Symbol	Representative of a sign. For example, notation of pitches or durations or tonal patterns or rhythm patterns. Symbols are read, whereas signs are audiated.
Symbolic Association-reading	A level of discrimination learning. At this level of learning students read familiar tonal patterns and rhythm patterns in familiar or unfamiliar order they have been taught at aural/oral and verbal association levels of learning.
Symbolic Association-writing	A level of discrimination learning. At this level of learning students learn to notate familiar tonal patterns and rhythm patterns in familiar or unfamiliar order they have been taught at aural/oral and verbal association levels of learning.
Syntax	Orderly arrangement of pitches and durations in a piece of music. Music has syntax (context), but not grammar.
Teaching Mode	When a teacher sings or chants with a student as the student performs an individual pattern in learning sequence activities.
Tempo	1) Speed at which rhythm patterns are performed and 2) Relative lengths of macrobeats within rhythm patterns.
Theoretical Understanding	Highest level of inference learning. Theoretical understanding includes three subparts: aural/oral, verbal, and symbolic. At this level of learning students learn theoretical information, such as the letter names of lines and spaces of the staff and time-value names of notes as they work with familiar and unfamiliar tonal patterns and rhythm patterns in unfamiliar order. At previous levels of learning, "what" and "how" are emphasized. "Why" is emphasized at the theoretical understanding level of learning.

Tie Pattern	One function of rhythm patterns. A tie pattern includes two patterns in which all or a portion of the final macrobeat in the first pair and all or a portion of the initial macrobeat of the second pair are connected (tied).
Time-Value Names	Arithmetic fraction names given to durations relative to a whole note seen in music notation.
Tonal Learning Sequence	Tonal learning sequence includes all tonal classifications and functions. Classifications and functions are taught sequentially in combination with skill learning sequence.
Tonal Pattern	Two, three, four, or five pitches in a given tonality audiated sequentially and forming a whole. Eight pitches in a diatonic scale comprise at least two tonal patterns.
Tonal Solfege	See tonal syllables
Tonal Syllables	Different names sung for different pitches in a tonal pattern. Tonal syllables used in learning sequence activities are based on the movable *do* system with a *la* based minor, not a *do* based minor.
Tonality	Determined by the resting tone. If *do* is the resting tone, tonality is major; if *la* is the resting tone, tonality is harmonic minor or Aeolian; if *re* is the resting tone, tonality is Dorian; if *mi* is the resting tone, tonality is Phrygian; if *fa* is the resting tone, tonality is Lydian; if *so* is the resting tone, tonality is Mixolydian; and if *ti* is the resting tone, tonality is Locrian. A tonality is always in a keyality but a keyality may not be in a tonality.
Tonic	Pitch name of keyality. For example, C, D, or E♭. Keyality has a tonic, whereas tonality has a resting tone.
Tonic Pattern	One function of tonal patterns. For example, in major tonality it includes an arrangement of "do mi so."

Triad	Three pitches sounded simultaneously.
Triple Meter	See usual triple meter.
Upbeat Pattern	One function of rhythm patterns. An upbeat pattern occurs prior to the beginning macrobeat of a rhythm pattern and it becomes part of the rhythm pattern it precedes.
Unfamiliar Order of Patterns	Familiar patterns not taught in specific order at levels of discrimination learning or familiar and unfamiliar patterns not taught in specific order at levels of inference learning. In inference learning, students deal with unfamiliar and familiar patterns, because the presence of unfamiliar patterns necessarily makes order unfamiliar.
Unfamiliar Patterns	Patterns learned at an inference level of learning.
Unusual Meter	Four types of meter in which macrobeats are of unequal length, regardless of whether they are audiated in pairs or more than a pair, whether some are intact, or whether they are divided into two or three microbeats of equal length.
Unusual Paired Intact Meter	Meter that results when macrobeats of unequal length are audiated in pairs and at least one macrobeat is intact.
Unusual Paired Meter	Meter that results when macrobeats of unequal length are audiated in pairs. Some macrobeats are divided into two and others into three microbeats of equal length.
Unusual Unpaired Intact Meter	Meter that results when macrobeats of uequal length are audiated in more than a pair and at least one macrobeat is intact.
Unusual Unpaired Meter	Meter that results when macrobeats of unequal length are audiated in more than a pair. Some macrobeats are divided into two and others into three microbeats of equal length.

Usual Combined Meter	Meter that results when macrobeats of equal length are audiated in pairs. Some macrobeats are divided into two and others into three microbeats of unequal length.
Usual Duple Meter	Meter that results when macrobeats of equal length are audiated in pairs. Macrobeats are divided into two microbeats of equal length.
Usual Meter	Three types of meter in which macrobeats of equal length are audiated in pairs. Macrobeats are divided into two or three microbeats of equal length or into two and three microbeats of unequal length, depending on meter.
Usual Triple Meter	Meter resulting when macrobeats of equal length are audiated in pairs. Macrobeats are divided into three microbeats of equal length.
Verbal Association	A level of discrimination learning. At this level of learning students learn a vocabulary of tonal patterns using tonal syllables and a vocabulary of rhythm patterns using rhythm syllables. The same patterns are taught at the aural/oral and verbal association levels. Proper names of classifications and functions are also learned at the verbal association level.
Vocabulary Names	See syllable names.
With Verbal Association	Use of tonal syllables or rhythm syllables in performing tonal patterns and rhythm patterns at the creativity/improvisation-aural/oral level of learning.
Without Verbal Association	Use of a neutral syllable in performing tonal patterns and rhythm patterns at the creativity/improvisation-aural/oral level of learning.

Biblography

Bernstein, L. (1966) *The Infinite Variety of Music*. New York: Simon and Schuster.

Bloom, B. (1964) *Stability and Change in Human Characteristics*. New York: John Wiley and Sons.

Bluestine, E. (2000) *The Ways Children Learn Music: An Introduction and Practical Guide to Music Learning Theory*. Chicago: GIA Publications, Inc.

Brand, M., ed. (1991) The Work of Edwin Gordon. *The Quarterly*, 2 (1 & 2), 3-147.

Donington, R. (1962) *The Interpretation of Early Music*. London: Faber and Faber.

Gagne, R. (1986) *The Conditions of Learning*. New York: Holt, Rinehart and Winston.

Gordon, E. E. (1971) *The Psychology of Music Teaching*. Englewood Cliffs: Prentice-Hall.

Gordon, E. E. (1976) *Tonal and Rhythm Patterns: An Objective Analysis*. Albany: State University of New York Press.

Gordon, E. E. (1978) *A Factor Analytic Description of Tonal and Rhythm Patterns and Objective Evidence of Pattern Difficulty Level and Growth Rate*. Chicago: GIA Publications.

Gordon, E. E. (1979) *Primary Measures of Music Audiation*. Chicago: GIA Publications.

Gordon, E. E. (1982) *Intermediate Measures of Music Audiation*. Chicago: GIA Publications.

Gordon, E. E. (1984) *Instrument Timbre Preference Test*. Chicago: GIA Publications.

Gordon, E. E. (1989) *Advanced Measures of Music Audiation*. Chicago: GIA Publications.

Gordon, E. E. (1989) *Audie*. Chicago: GIA Publications.

Gordon, E. E. (1990) *Tonal Register Books One and Two*. Chicago: GIA Publications.

Gordon, E. E. (1990) *Rhythm Register Books One and Two*. Chicago: GIA Publications.

Gordon, E. E. (1990) *A Music Learning Theory for Newborn and Young Children*. Chicago: GIA Publications.

Gordon, E. E. (1991) *Tonal and Rhythm Pattern Audiation Cassettes*. Chicago: GIA Publications.

Gordon, E. E. (1991) A Response to volume 2, numbers 1 & 2 of The Quarterly. *The Quarterly* 2. 4 62-72.

Gordon, E. E., Bolton, B., Hicks, W., & Taggart, C. C. (1993) *Songs and Chants Without Words*. Chicago: GIA Publications.

Gordon, E. (1995) *Musical Aptitude Profile*. Chicago: GIA Publications.

Gordon, E. E., Bolton, B., Taggart, C. C., Valerio, W. H., & Reynolds, A. (1997) *Jump Right In: The Music Curriculum*. Chicago: GIA Publications.

Gordon, E. E. (1998) *Harmonic Improvisation Readiness Record and Rhythm Improvisation Readiness Record*. Chicago: GIA Publications.

Gordon, E. E. (1998) *Introduction to Research and the Psychology of Music*. Chicago: GIA Publications.

Gordon, E. E. (2000) *Rhythm: Contrasting the Implications of Audiation and Notation*. Chicago: GIA Publications.

Gordon, E. E. (2000) *Music Aptitude and Related Tests: An Introduction*. Chicago: GIA Publications.

Gordon, E. E. (2000) *More Songs and Chants Without Words*. Chicago: GIA Publications.

Gordon, E. E. (2001) *Reference Handbook for Using Learning Sequence Activities*. Chicago: GIA Publications.

Gordon, E. E. (2003) *Improvisation in the Music Classroom*. Chicago: GIA Publications.

Gordon, E.E. (2003) *Music Audiation Games*. Chicago: GIA Publications.

Gordon, E.E. (2004) *The Aural/Visual Experience of Music Literacy: Reading and Writing Music Notation*. Chicago: GIA Publications.

Gordon, E. E. (2005) *Harmonic Improvisation for Adult Musicians*. Chicago: GIA Publications.

Gordon, E. E. (2007) *Learning Sequences in Music. A Contemporary Music Learning Theory*. Chicago: GIA Publications.

Gordon, E. E. (2007) *Lecture Series for Learning Sequences in Music. A Contemporary Music Learning Theory*. Chicago: GIA Publications.

Grunow, R. F., Gordon, E. E. Azzara, C. D. & Martin, M. E. (1989) *Jump Right In: The Instrumental Series*. Chicago: GIA Publications.

Harnoncourt, N. (1989) *Baroque Music Today: Music as Speech. Ways to a New Understanding of Music*. trans. O'Neill, M. Portland, Oregon; Amadeus Press.

Houle, George. (1987) *Meter in Music, 1600-1800*. Bloomington: Indiana University Press.

Jaques-Dalcroze, E. (1967) *Rhythm, Music and Education*. trans. Rubenstein, H. F. London: Riverside Press.

Jordan, J. (1996) *Evoking Sound: Fundamentals of Choral Conducting and Rehearsing*. Chicago: GIA Publications.

Laban, R. (1971) *Mastery of Movement*. London: MacDonald and Evans.

Lange, D. M. (2005) *Together in Harmony: Combining Orff Schulwerk and Music Learning Theory*. Chicago: GIA Publications.

Leinsdorf, E. (1981) *The Composer's Advocate*. New Haven: Yale University Press.

Lowe, M. (2004) *Music Moves for Piano*. Chicago: GIA Publications.

Loulié, É. (1965) *Elements or Principles of Music*. trans. A. Cohen. NewYork: Institute of Mediaeval Music.

Rainbow, B. (1967) *The Land Without Music*. London: Novello.

Rainbow, B. (1990) *Music in Educational Thought and Practice*. Aberystwyth, Dyfed, Wales: Boethius Press.

Runfola, M. & Taggart, C. C., eds. (2005) *The Development and Practical Application of Music Learning Theory*. Chicago: GIA Publications.

Seashore, C. E. (1919) *The Psychology of Musical Talent*. New York: Silver Burdett.

Seymour, H. A. (1915) *How to Think Music*. New York: G. Schirmer.

Thurmond, J. M. (1982) *Note Grouping*. Camp Hill, Pennsylvania: JMT Publications.

Tomatis, A. A. (1996) *The Ear and Language*. Noraul, Ontario, Canada: Moulin Publishing Company.

Vygotsky, L. S. (1967) *Thought and Language*. eds. and trans. Haufmann, E. & Vakar, G. Cambridge: MIT Press.

Vygotsky, L. S. (1978) *Mind in Society*. eds. Cole, M., John-Steiner, V., Scribner, S. & Souberman, E. Cambridge: Harvard University Press.

Zuckerkandl, V. (1956) *Sound and Symbol*. trans. Trask, W. R. New York: Pantheon Books.

Zuckerkandl, V. (1973) *Man the Musician*. trans. Guterman, N. Princeton, New Jersey: Princeton University Press.

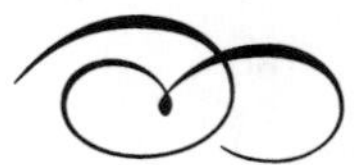

Index